praying
from the
gut

an honest prayer journal
for teens

All Scripture quotations, unless otherwise indicated, are taken from the *Holy Bible*, New Living Translation, copyright © 1996. Used by permission of Tyndale House Publishers, Inc., Wheaton, Illinois 60189. All rights reserved.
All Scripture quotations marked NIV are taken from the HOLY BIBLE, NEW INTERNATIONAL VERSION®. NIV®. Copyright © 1973, 1978, 1984 by International Bible Society. Used by permission of Zondervan Publishing House. All rights reserved.

Cover photo by Getty Images
Cover and interior design by Robert Glover
Edited by Dale Reeves
Typesetting by Andrew Quach

Library of Congress Cataloging-in-Publication Data:
James, Steven, 1969-
    Praying from the gut : an honest prayer journal for teens / Steven James.—1st American pbk. ed.
       p. cm.
    ISBN 0-7847-1334-0 (pbk.)
1. Teenagers—Prayer-books and devotions—English. I. Title.
BV4850.J34 2004
242'.83—dc22

2004001926

Standard Publishing, Cincinnati, Ohio.
A Division of Standex International Corporation.

11	10	09	08	07	06	05	04
7	6	5	4	3	2	1	

ISBN: 0-7847-1334-0

praying
from the
gut

an honest prayer journal
for teens

steven james

EMPOWERED® Youth Products
Standard Publishing
Cincinnati, Ohio

dedication

This book is dedicated to Todd Huhn, doctor, microbiologist, air force captain, actor, gourmet chef, martial artist, illusionist, brother and friend.

acknowledgments

Special thanks to Liesl Huhn and Dana Standridge for editorial insight, for challenging my assumptions, doing endless hours of research, and for sharing their ideas about how to pray like a girl; to Dale Reeves for believing in this book; to Grace Fellowship Church for the inspiration to go deeper and further; and to the kind folks at Doe River Gorge Ministries for giving me a place to get away from the frantic pace of life and focus on my own relationship with God.

contents

prayers of truth

prayers for girls

prayers for guys

introduction

SURE, we talk to God.

Maybe we mumble a few words of thanks before dinner. Or we whisper a short prayer at bedtime. Some of us hold hands in a circle and pray around our flagpoles. We may even talk to God off and on throughout the day. Yeah, we pray. We talk to God.

And yet, most of the time it's a joke. Most of the time it's not deep or honest stuff at all. It's just a habit or a ritual.

Few of us are ever really *honest* with God. We say the prayers we were taught as kids:

"Come, Lord Jesus, be our guest. Let these gifts to us be blest. Amen."

*"Now I lay me down to sleep, I pray the Lord my soul to keep,
If I should die before I wake, I pray the Lord my soul to take."*

Or, maybe the most honest one of all:
"Good food. Good meat. Good God. Let's eat!"

But if the truth were known (and with God it always is), most of us wear masks. Most of us spend our lives piling on more and more layers of protection against the real world. We pray for the things we think we're supposed to pray for. We say the words we've heard others say. We chant or repeat or nod our heads without ever really opening up the secret places of our hearts. Sometimes it's all a show to impress others with how spiritual we are. Sometimes we just go through the motions.

An honest look at the Psalms, a collection of Jewish prayers found in the Bible, reveals that the authors of those prayers were brutally honest. They called it like they saw it—sometimes cursing their enemies . . . sometimes baring their souls by confessing terrible sins . . . sometimes losing themselves in radiant praise of God's majesty . . . and Jesus was just as honest and desperate as he cried out to God from the cross, "My God! My God! Why have you forsaken me?!"

But somewhere over the years, we've lost sight of that gut-level, honest communication with God. We seem to be afraid that if we really let God know how we feel, what we think or where we hurt, he'll somehow be surprised, disappointed or let down. But exactly the opposite is true! The thing that God desires most from us is that we stop hiding once and for all and come to him in complete honesty and humility.

God is the only one who sees us as we really are—down to the core of our being—and loves us anyway.

This book will bridge the gap between the honest, ancient teachings of the Bible and the postmodern, hyper-driven, techno culture of today. Each prayer is an honest look at a different area of your life that you often keep hidden from God. And each prayer includes what you can say to God instead.

so what kinds of prayers are these?

Groans. Screams. Voiced tears. Explosive praise or humble joys or shattered dreams of broken hearts. From confession to hope, and grief to praise, these prayers will allow you to open up your emotions to God.

Praying isn't so much about the words you say, it's the attitude you choose. Don't worry if you can't think of what to say. God's Spirit has a vocabulary that covers all your needs. Approaching God isn't a ceremony. You don't need a priest or a hymnbook or a church service or a bunch of candles burning on the windowsills. Just an honest heart.

Tell him those dark and hidden secrets, open up those shadowy corners of your heart that you so carefully keep hidden from everyone else. Lay bare your hidden vices and shameful memories.

Your secrets, your failures and those things you think no one else should know—tell those to God. After all, he won't heal what you won't give him. Express your anger, admit your mistakes, accept his grace. Be real.

Beg for his presence. Tell him what you wish would happen to that kid that makes fun of you, or how much you wanna have sex with your girlfriend. Ask him what you're supposed to do about your eating disorder, or your homework, or your athlete's foot or your acne scars. Nothing is too big and nothing is too small to bring to God.

When you don't feel anything toward God, tell him that. God already knows your heart, your sins, your regrets, your shame, your mistakes. Your prayers don't suddenly shock God. He's not like, "Whoa! I'm sure glad she told me that! I never knew that she struggled with gossiping before!"

God already knows all there is to know about you! He's just waiting for you to acknowledge that *you* know. And that you need him. And that you'll turn to him in everything because you trust him for answers.

If you're a little rusty being totally honest with God, this book will help oil the hinges of your heart as you open yourself up to him. Use these prayers to prime the pump, then let your own words and emotions flow toward your heavenly Father.

Before you get started, you should know that some of the prayers in this book won't necessarily apply to what you're going through in your life right now. It might be best to flip through the table of contents and choose a couple of prayers that really speak to where you're at and what you're going through right now. Read those first and then move on from there. But however you choose to read this book, be sure to take the time to let God know what's really going on in your heart.

If you're used to most church prayers you might notice that the word "Amen" doesn't appear at the end of any of the prayers in this book. "Amen" means "so shall it be," or "that's the way it is, dude." It's a way of saying that God is in control. And it's an agreement with him that he'll hear and answer your prayer.

None of the prayers in this book are intended to be the final word on a subject. Instead, just use them to open up the conversation between you and God. Finish the prayer in your own words and your own way by being authentic and open with God. Then, when you're done, tell him "Amen" in whatever way makes sense to you.

Open up. Be honest with God. Don't hold back. Pray from the head, believing that God is listening. Pray from the heart, trusting that he cares about your life. And pray from the gut, letting him in on your deepest struggles, questions, fears and doubts.

He's available. He's listening. And he's waiting for you to talk to him right now.

prayers
of
need

JESUS didn't always see eye to eye with his parents—well, at least his mom and his stepdad, Joseph. He walked so in-step with his true Father, God, that he got into trouble with Mary and Joseph once when they all went to Jerusalem.

Jesus was twelve at the time. He'd gone to Jerusalem with his parents to celebrate the Jewish Passover festival. When the holiday was over, his parents took off for home. They figured Jesus was with some of the relatives.

But he wasn't. So, after three days of searching for him, they finally went back, exasperated, to the Jerusalem temple. And that's where they found him. He'd spent the last few days there talking with the religious leaders and asking them probing questions about God.

And of course, Mary and Joseph were upset:

His parents didn't know what to think. "Son!" his mother said to him. "Why have you done this to us? Your father and I have been frantic, searching for you everywhere."

"But why did you need to search?" he asked. "You should have known that I would be in my Father's house." But they didn't understand what he meant. (Luke 2:48-50)

This is the only place Mary referred to Joseph as Jesus' father. She forgot his true father was God! And in Jesus' reply to her, there's a gentle rebuke, "You should have known that I would be in my Father's house." And even though she didn't understand the depth of meaning of those words, she got the point. She never again refers to her husband as Jesus' father.

This is a classic case of two parents not understanding their son. Mary forgot who Jesus' real father was. If Mary would've known Jesus better, she would've understood his priorities, identity and mission in life. And right away she would've understood his talk about being in his Father's house.

Go to Jesus when you feel like your parents just don't understand you. He knows exactly how you feel.

from the gut

Man. My parents just don't understand what it's like being a teenager today. I mean, how could they be more clueless!

Jesus, did you ever get annoyed with your parents? I mean, I know your mom was cool and everything, but you must have wondered what she was doing sometimes, right? You must have been totally fed up with her sometimes, right? I mean, she really didn't understand your whole mission until after you came back from the dead! I mean, they took off and left you in the city for three days! How did you put up with Joseph and her? How did you survive dealing with your parents without going totally insane?!

It's like I'm never good enough or smart enough or polite enough and my room is never clean enough to make 'em happy. It's like they expect me to be perfect or something!

Sometimes, they act like idiots in front of my friends. And some days I could swear they're from another world!

But the thing is—and I know you'll understand this—I still care about 'em. It's hard for me to show 'em that I care, or tell 'em that I do, but I do.

I don't know what I'm trying to say. It's just tough because I want 'em to like me, but we just don't seem to connect. It's almost like we're from two totally different planets. Like we talk two totally different languages. At least you live in both those worlds and you speak both our languages. Bridge the gap, Jesus. And help us to get along. Somehow . . .

JESUS, can you understand what it's like to look at someone else's life and see so much stuff that you wish was in yours? Can you understand what it's like to look at 'em and wish you had their life? They seem so happy and popular and their lives look so easy and carefree—so perfect—compared to mine.

I know it can't really be as good as it looks on the outside, but well . . . that's how I feel. And it makes me ashamed to say this, but the truth is, I'm not really happy about who I am.

It seems like I'm never satisfied with who I am. I'm always comparing myself to others to try and feel good about myself because I wanna see how I measure up. I'm sure you're never jealous. At least not jealous like I am. I mean I know you get annoyed when we honor and praise and worship other things above you. I guess that's a type of jealousy, but I'm talking about the other kind. The selfish kind of jealousy.

I need you to help me feel content with who I am!

Forgive me for thinking about myself so much. Help me to be satisfied with simply knowing you. After all, that's the only thing that's really gonna last. I mean, popularity will fade away, riches won't last, even money evaporates. But my relationship with you lasts forever.

And even if I have you and nothing else I'm still better off than someone who has everything in the world except you. Help me to know that. Really know it and live it.

And help me to see my life through your eyes rather than my own. Thanks . . .

"Do not wish to be anything but what you are, and try to be that perfectly."
—st. francis de sales (1567-1622), bishop of geneva

> "To be nobody but yourself in a world which is doing its best, night and day, to make you everybody else—means to fight the hardest battle which any human being can fight; and never stop fighting."
>
> —e. e. cummings (1894-1962), poet

from the heart

sometimes i wish i had this person's life . . .

_____

_____

_____

when i get jealous of other people, remind me that . . .

_____

_____

_____

when i'm not content, remind me to rely on you for . . .

_____

_____

_____

deeper and further

There were times when Jesus wished things were different in his life. In the Garden of Gethsemane when he saw the cross ahead, he asked God to send a different set of circumstances into his life. Read Matthew 26:38, 39 to find out what Jesus cared about even more than avoiding the upcoming suffering. Into whose hands did Jesus place his future? How does the example of Jesus affect your life today?

"So if we have enough food and clothing, let us be content."

1 Timothy 6:8

"You can ask for anything in my name, and I will do it, because the work of the Son brings glory to the Father. Yes, ask anything in my name, and I will do it!"
—Jesus of nazareth (john 14:13, 14)

from the gut

DID you really mean that, Jesus? Did you really mean we can ask for anything in your name and you'll give it to us? Anything?

Well, okay then. I need more money. I need more cash.

Now, I wanna be careful so I'm not asking this for the wrong reasons. Send your Spirit down and give me wisdom to figure out where my desire for money is coming from. If it's coming from me (just so I can get more stuff that doesn't matter to you) then kill that desire right here and now. I don't wanna fill my life with stuff that's gonna come between us.

But if the desire for more money is because there's a real need in my life, then keep your promise. Give me what I'm asking for in your name.

Jesus, you know my real needs. There are so many things that I think I need but I don't really need at all. In fact, I'd have to say that most of the stuff I desire isn't stuff I need at all, it's just stuff I want. Show me the difference. Provide for my needs, not my greeds.

I don't wanna store up treasures here on earth, I wanna store 'em up in Heaven where I'm gonna spend eternity with you. I don't want money for security, 'cause I want to rely on you for that. And I don't want to be greedy 'cause I know greed only leads people farther away from you.

But I also don't want to feel guilty coming to you when I have a real need in my life.

And right now my need is for more money.

How much? How much money do I need? Well, enough so that I'm not always envying other people and scheming how to get more, but yet not so much that I start to let it become my god. I'll trust you to know the difference and do what's right.

So, there you go. Sort out my motives and provide for my needs. Thanks for listening . . .

> "People think we make $3 million and $4 million a year. They don't realize that most of us only make $500,000."
>
> —pete incaviglia, baseball player, 1990

from the heart

here's why i feel like i need more money now . . .

_____
_____
_____
_____
_____

here are three things that are more important than money . . .

1. _____
2. _____
3. _____

here's what i'll do with the money when you provide it . . .

_____
_____
_____
_____
_____

"No man is rich who shakes and groans convinced that he needs more."
—anicius manlius severinus boethius (480-524),
christian philosopher, poet and politician

"I'd give a thousand bucks to be one of them millionaires."
—an anonymous truck driver

deeper and further

Jesus often warned about loving the things of this world and thereby neglecting nurturing your relationship with God. Read Luke 12:20. What does Jesus call someone who focuses on earthly wealth and neglects his relationship with God? Why is this such a hard warning to follow? What's your priority? Does anything need to change in your life?

"But godliness with contentment is great gain. For we brought nothing into the world, and we can take nothing out of it."
1 Timothy 6:6, 7 NIV

TURN on the TV, flip open the newspaper, tune into the radio and you'll be reminded that you live in a violent world. Stabbings. Shootings. Murder. Rape. Chemical weapons. Nuclear weapons. Rogue nations. Terrorism. It's almost enough to make you lose hope. On the big scale, countries are constantly positioning themselves against each other. On a smaller scale, none of us knows what personal tragedy tomorrow might bring into our lives. A car wreck. A life-threatening illness. A disabling accident.

Jesus might not have worried like we do about the future, but he certainly knew what it was to live in an uncertain world. He faced violent crowds, was betrayed by a close friend and watched his supporters run away. He was falsely accused, beaten, tortured, mocked and killed. He felt lonely and completely abandoned.

Jesus understands the desperation and helplessness we feel at the hands of injustice and violence. Look at what he told his followers before returning to Heaven:

Peace I leave with you; my peace I give you. I do not give to you as the world gives. Do not let your hearts be troubled and do not be afraid. (John 14:27 NIV)

When you call out to him, Jesus may choose to calm your storm, or he may choose to just calm your soul instead. God's comfort looks different at different times. But God's comfort always grows—only grows—from the assurance of his presence. So take the time to reflect on God's power, presence and promises rather than keeping your eyes on the swirling, storming world all around you. God doesn't change. Everything else in the world does.

When you lean on God for support, he won't let you down. He'll stand by you through all the questions, fears and doubts. Commit yourself to him. You'll find him to be the strongest helper of all when you need him the most.

The future seems so uncertain, God. We've been at war, our troops are stationed all around the globe and terrorists continue to plot against our country.

I mean, there's all that trouble in the Middle East, suicide bombers and nations with nuclear weapons pointed at our throats. And of course, accidents happen—car wrecks and stuff. And it's like, I don't even know if I'm gonna be alive tomorrow. But you will, right? You're still in control, aren't you? Sometimes I gotta say, I wonder. It doesn't look like it sometimes.

Some people say we're living in uncertain times—but when have the times ever been certain? Never. The only certainty in this life is that it's gonna end with death—unless you come first, that is.

God, I need you to comfort me. Calm my fears, give me security in your promises and reliance on your strength. It's so easy to forget that you're in control. It's so easy to let fear and worry cloud my mind.

I'm not asking that you make my life easy, just that you fill up more of my heart with your strength and presence and comfort. Jesus, didn't you call the Holy Spirit the Comforter? Well, that's what I need right now, more comfort. More of the Holy Spirit's comfort. The times might be uncertain, but your comfort isn't. That's guaranteed.

Do something today to show me that you've still got a hold of this crazy, cruel world . . .

"It is sad to think that the first few people on earth needed no books, movies, games or music to inspire cold-blooded murder. The day that Cain bashed his brother Abel's brains in, the only motivation he needed was his own human disposition to violence. Times have not become more violent. They've just become more televised."
—marilyn manson, rock star (quoted in ROLLING STONE magazine, 5/28/99)

from the heart

these are the things i worry about the most . . .

_____
_____
_____
_____

this is why it's so hard for me not to worry about tomorrow . . .

_____
_____
_____
_____

these are the three biggest needs that i have in my life right now . . .

1. _____
_____
_____

2. _____
_____
_____

3. _____
_____
_____

Why do people worry? What does worry have to say about our level of faith in God? What's the secret to overcoming fear and worry about tomorrow? Read Matthew 6:25-34. What insights about life does Jesus point out to prove we shouldn't worry? How will these verses affect your life?

"Don't be afraid of those who want to kill you. They can only kill your body; they cannot touch your soul. Fear only God, who can destroy both soul and body in hell. Not even a sparrow, worth only half a penny, can fall to the ground without your Father knowing it. And the very hairs on your head are all numbered. So don't be afraid; you are more valuable to him than a whole flock of sparrows."

Matthew 10:28-31

THERE are lots of reasons to feel restless. Sometimes it seems like our circumstances are holding us back from pursuing our dreams. Sometimes no one else seems to understand where we're coming from. Sometimes it's boredom. Other times it's simply frustration with the stupidity of the world.

Hebrews 11 lists a number of believers who were content to follow God, but were never content on this planet. They longed for something far better:

All these faithful ones died without receiving what God had promised them, but they saw it all from a distance and welcomed the promises of God. They agreed that they were no more than foreigners and nomads here on earth. And obviously people who talk like that are looking forward to a country they can call their own. If they had meant the country they came from, they would have found a way to go back. But they were looking for a better place, a heavenly homeland. (Hebrews 11:13-16)

This planet, with all of its pain and problems and heartaches and despair, isn't how we're supposed to spend eternity. We were made to enjoy God's presence and experience intimacy with the Almighty. So it's no wonder we spend our restless lives searching for more satisfaction than this life can offer.

Lasting contentment will never come in this life. In fact, the Bible calls all believers aliens and strangers on this planet because we're just passing through on our way to get home. If you feel restless it may not be a bad thing. It might mean that you're really longing for the life you were meant to live all along.

God, sometimes it seems like this world just doesn't fit me. I long for something more. More adventure and freedom and happiness and truth in my heart. It's like something is calling me forward into the unknown, past who I am, to something more. I feel the call beyond what I know and what I can control to a deeper, bigger life than I've ever experienced or dreamed of before.

I'm restless with my life! Could it be you who is calling to me? Could it be your Spirit that's beckoning me? If so, here I am! Lead me on into the great adventure! Show me the freedom of the frontier and the adventure that lies beyond the horizon.

Expand me, Lord. Blow apart the tediousness and boredom of each day and let your Spirit explode within me, showering me with new truths about you and new grace for my soul and new directions for my life.

Wake me up to the adventure of knowing and following you!

Help me to not be content in this world, but to always yearn for something more, something greater, something lasting and forever. Help me to not be content with a little of your Spirit, a little of obedience, a little of love. Instead, help me to always desire more of you. But God, let me be content with what you decide to give me on this side of Heaven, instead of being led around by the frantic desire for more, more, more—for newer stuff and a better job and cooler friends and more money. Teach me to be content.

Let my restlessness grow from a deep desire to be closer to you and to the world to come, rather than a desperate clinging to this temporary and fragile world. I don't wanna get distracted by the glittery delights of this life. I wanna walk in faith like those Bible heroes listed in Hebrews 11. And I wanna start today . . .

> "But what, you ask, of earth? Earth, I think, will not be found by anyone to be in the end a very distinct place. I think earth, if chosen instead of Heaven, will turn out to have been, all along, only a region in Hell: and earth, if put second to Heaven, to have been from the beginning a part of Heaven itself."
>
> —c. s. lewis (1898-1963), THE GREAT DIVORCE

from the heart

God, help me long for these types of things . . .

_____
_____
_____
_____
_____
_____

when i get restless, help me to remember these promises about Heaven . . .

_____
_____
_____
_____
_____

teach me to long for the right things in life; stuff like . . .

_____
_____
_____
_____
_____
_____

deeper and further

How content should believers become in this life? How comfortable should we be? Paul writes about a guy named Demas who got restless waiting on God's calling and became distracted by the things of this world. Read 2 Timothy 4:9-11 to find out what happened to him. What does the story of Demas have to do with your life today?

"Though you have not seen him, you love him; and even though you do not see him now, you believe in him and are filled with an inexpressible and glorious joy."

1 Peter 1:8 NIV

GOD, there's so much going on in my life! I feel like the walls are closing in on me! I am so stressed!

Help!

Things are moving so fast I don't even know how to keep up and I feel all this pressure that I need to be successful and get into a good college and get a good job and make money and if I don't do well now then my whole future is gonna be flushed down the drain.

I've got deadlines at school and pressure from my parents and things could be better between me and my friends. And I never seem to have enough time or money or patience.

I don't know how some people can handle their lives without freaking out! I mean, there's gotta be a good way to deal with all this stress, but I don't know what it is. I mean, it's just too much to handle! I try dealing with one thing and then something else always comes up and I can never escape it all. And I never feel I'm ever caught up with anything.

God, I know you're in charge of the universe. I know you're in control of everything. You're the one calling the shots. So, cut me some slack! Teach me what to do! Help me to relax and lean on you instead of on myself when I get all stressed out like this . . .

"Every night, I have to read a book, so that my mind will stop thinking about things that I stress about."

—britney spears, pop singer

from the heart

here's why i'm so stressed . . .

_____

_____

_____

these are the people putting the most pressure on me . . .

_____

_____

_____

here's what i'll do to rely more on you . . .

_____

_____

_____

deeper and further

Sometimes we try to do too much. When Moses was overworked and stressed out (read Exodus 18:13-27) his father-in-law suggested that he spread the work around. That alone solved most of his problem. Is there something you're trying to do that you don't need to be doing? Is there something you could let go of or someone you need to talk to? Will you?

"Give your burdens to the LORD, and he will take care of you."
                                                                      Psalm 55:22

OKAY, I'm gonna be honest here—I know I'm supposed to do it. I know I'm supposed to believe that you hear me and that you care about me and I know I'm supposed to trust that you're gonna answer all my prayers, but . . . well, it's just that right now I'm not sure what to believe. And I can't seem to get motivated to pray about my needs at all or even get the right words out.

Part of me is just sick and tired of it all. And part of me just doesn't care.

Now, God, I know you could get really mad at me for telling you all this stuff, but I don't think you will. 'Cause I'm just being as honest as I can. And I need to talk to you about it, I know that much. But I'm not really sure what to say.

I know you don't want me to go through the motions of the spiritual life if it's not really from a believing heart. I know that. So, hear the stuff I don't know how to say. Hear the longings of my soul and the groans that I don't even know how to put into words.

Help me, God. Change me. Give me a passion for you that isn't easily quenched. Give me an experience of your love that takes my desire for you far beyond words. Give me a faith in you that isn't easily shaken. And give me such conviction about you that even if I don't feel like saying anything to you, I can still seek you, rest in your presence and respond to your calling in my life . . .

> "We have to pray with our eyes on God, not on the difficulties."
> —oswald chambers (1874-1917), author of the classic devotional
> MY UTMOST FOR HIS HIGHEST

from the heart

here's why i'm not too much into praying these days . . .

_____

_____

_____

here's how i wish my prayer life was like . . .

_____

_____

_____

here's the thing i'd like to pray about the most, if i could . . .

_____

_____

_____

deeper and further

Look up Romans 8:26. Does this verse sound like it applies to your relationship with God? Why or why not? How does it make you feel to find out that God doesn't even expect you to come up with the right words when you're praying? How does that change your attitude concerning prayer? Why is it freeing to find out that the Spirit, not you, is responsible for finding the right way to express your prayers?

"And so I tell you, keep on asking, and you will be given what you ask for. Keep on looking, and you will find. Keep on knocking, and the door will be opened. For everyone who asks, receives. Everyone who seeks, finds. And the door is opened to everyone who knocks."

Luke 11:9, 10

THERE are lots of places to hide in this world. Addictions. Ecstasy. Booze. Porn. Marijuana. I've met people who've hidden so much and for so long they don't even know how to come out and face the real world again. They're hidden so deep they've lost themselves.

There are lots of easy answers to big problems. People turn to suicide when they're in despair, abortion when they're confused and sex when they're alone. It's like there are all these voices calling out, "Come over here! You can have a sweet escape. I'll make your dreams come true. I'll solve your problems. Trust me. Give yourself to me!" But the voices are lies and their "answers" are only land mines for your soul.

I don't wanna hide and I don't want easy answers. But, it's not easy to say "no" to all that stuff. And sometimes, I get tired of saying "no" and I want to say "yes."

So what am I gonna do? It seems so natural to want to escape my problems. How come they're so big? How come there aren't any answers in sight? How come it's so tempting to look for an easy way out?

God, I'm tempted to get addicted to something, anything—everything!—but you. Show me another way. A way to face my problems with you by my side. Rather than running or hiding or trying to escape. Show me a better way. Show me your way. The way of truth rather than denial. The way of openness, rather than escape. The way of peace and trust rather than confusion. Here's my hand. Here's my heart. Lead me, God, out of these problems and closer to your heart . . .

from the heart

these are the things i usually do to try and escape my problems . . .

_____

_____

_____

if i stop hiding i'll have to start . . .

_____

_____

_____

here's the first step i'll take toward facing my problems . . .

_____

_____

_____

deeper and further

Nobody likes the idea of having to go through tough times. Why do you think God lets us get to the point where we feel so desperate for a way to escape? What purpose do you think he has in mind for all that? Read Luke 13:1-9. Jesus used the example of senseless suffering to urge people to do what? Take a few moments to search your heart to see if there are some choices you need to make to walk more in line with God's will.

Then make them.

"The Sovereign LORD, the Holy One of Israel, says, 'Only in returning to me and waiting for me will you be saved. In quietness and confidence is your strength.'"

Isaiah 30:15

JESUS faced periods of great stress in his ministry. And even though he never hurried or rushed around hassled and worried and fretting about how things were gonna work out, there were times when he was extremely busy and overwhelmed.

Early in his ministry, Jesus showed his remarkable power by healing people. One night, huge crowds from all over the region came to his door. He responded by having compassion on them. He healed the sick and ordered demons to come out of their victims. As a result, the people wouldn't leave him alone even for a few minutes. So what did Jesus do?

> *The next morning Jesus awoke long before daybreak and went out alone into the wilderness to pray. Later Simon and the others went out to find him. They said, "Everyone is asking for you."*
> *But he replied, "We must go on to other towns as well, and I will preach to them, too, because that is why I came." (Mark 1:35-38)*

Jesus took time to get away from all the business and to reconnect with his heavenly Father. Then, when they came looking for him to get him back into the same busy schedule, Jesus stuck to his guns and went in the direction that God was leading him into. He could have settled in there and kept healing. There was certainly plenty of ministry to do! But instead, he went where God called him and unashamedly embraced God's calling for his life.

When we're overwhelmed, we need to reconnect with God, reprioritize our lives and stay focused on God's calling for us, too. Just like Jesus did.

from the gut

God, life is too big for me right now.
It's just too much for me!

My commitments are spinning out of control and I don't know where to turn and I have all these friendships to maintain and appointments to keep and all this homework to do and I haven't had a chance to pray or read my Bible or just BE for weeks.

Life just seems to pull me in so many directions these days. School. Work. Family. TV. Sports. Internet. Cheerleading. Video games. Relationships. Personal time. There just isn't enough time in the day for everything, and to top it all off, the things I really care about—my friends, my dreams, adventure, joy, love, you—I never seem to have any energy left to pursue that kind of stuff.

I'm tempted to ask you to change my circumstances. I'm tempted to ask you to stretch more hours into the day or something like that. So I can get more stuff done or catch up somehow or deal with life better.

But I'm not gonna ask that. I'm not even gonna ask that you make all my problems go away. Instead, just give me the courage to do what I know is right—help me give up the things that don't belong in my life. Give me the guts to say "no" to the people who keep asking me to do more than I can. And walk with me each step of the way.

Help me, God. Life's too big for me, but it's not too big for you. Thanks . . .

"Obstacles are those frightful things you see when you take your eyes off your goal."

—henry ford (1863-1947), automobile pioneer

from the heart

God, this is why i feel so overwhelmed . . .

_____

_____

_____

_____

_____

_____

here are some of the things i don't really need in my life right now . . .

_____

_____

_____

_____

_____

here's what i'll do the next time i feel overwhelmed . . .

_____

_____

_____

_____

_____

Flip your Bible open to Psalm 18. David cries out to God in verse 6, he writes about God's answer in verses 17-20 and then he records his response in verse 49. What do these verses tell you about how you should pray and respond to God? How do they apply to your life right now?

"From the ends of the earth, I will cry out to you for help, for my heart is overwhelmed. Lead me to the towering rock of safety, for you are my safe refuge, a fortress where my enemies cannot reach me."
Psalm 61:2, 3

rescue me

O GOD, life is swirling around me so fast I think I'm gonna drown! I need your hope. And I need your help.

Jesus, I long for more of you in my life—more of your grace, more of your power, more of your peace, more of your presence. More of you in my spirit and heart and mind and will.

On the one hand, Lord, I know that sounds kinda weird since you're already totally present and here with me. But I guess there's too much of me in the way right now.

Change it! Burn away all that doesn't belong. Tear out of my heart all the alluring attractions and deadly diversions and evil enticements of this world! O God, let me see the reality of your presence more clearly—crystal clearly!

I seek the truth, God, whatever that means and wherever that journey takes me. I know the road won't be easy because it'll be filled with honest repentance and confessions that I won't wanna make. You'll show me things I won't really want to see. You'll reveal things to me that I'd rather not know. But all of that will draw me closer as you show me more and more of the truth. And more and more of yourself.

I know that an honest life will require me to give up my secret longings for fame and fortune. But God, I will! I will!

I want you alone! Give me a passion for your presence! Overwhelm me with your grace. Fill me with your Spirit and cover me with your power. I'm here. I'm ready. I'm open to your call . . .

refresh me

O Lord, my soul is a desert, parched and thirsty and praying for rain. Let your grace fall upon me! Let the showers of your love land on my heart! I will drink them in! I will open myself to receive all that you give!

The sun has been scorching me far too long! The sands have been dusty and dry and longing for rain much too long. Here I am! Here I await. And now, on the horizon, I can see the clouds, your clouds, beginning to gather and form.

As the wind of your presence begins blowing gently and freely in my soul once again . . .

"As the storm still seeks its end in peace when it strikes against peace with all its might, even thus my rebellion strikes against thy love and still its cry is—I want thee, only thee."

—rabindranath tagore (1861-1941) indian poet, playwright, painter, novelist and winner of the 1913 nobel prize in literature

from the heart

here are three of the things that've been getting between us lately . . .

1. _____
_____
_____

2. _____
_____
_____

3. _____
_____
_____

even when i can't feel you close, i'll remind myself of your love by . . .

_____
_____
_____
_____

here's what i would compare your presence to . . .

_____

_____

_____

_____

deeper and further

Read Psalm 139. How does it make you feel to find out that no matter where you go, God will already be there waiting for you? How does that change your perspective? How does it change your attitude? How does it affect the very concept of being alone? Why do you say that?

"If I ride the wings of the morning, if I dwell by the farthest oceans, even there your hand will guide me, and your strength will support me. I could ask the darkness to hide me and the light around me to become night—but even in darkness I cannot hide from you."

Psalm 139:9-12

prayers of pain

LIFE wasn't easy for Jesus.

At the beginning of his life, his mom and stepdad couldn't find lodging so Jesus was born in a feeding trough for animals. Then, even as a baby, the king of the land tried to have him killed. After Mary and Joseph escaped with the baby Jesus to Egypt, they lived there as foreigners until the king died and they could return safely to Israel.

As Jesus grew up, his family didn't have lots of influence or lots of money.

And when Jesus became a traveling preacher, he didn't exactly strike it rich. On top of that, he made enemies with the most powerful Jewish leaders almost everywhere he went. People didn't know what to make of Jesus. Some called him a drunk, others thought he might be demon-possessed or insane. Throughout his ministry there were numerous attempts at his life.

He was betrayed by one of his closest friends, abandoned by the guys who promised to stick with him no matter what and misunderstood by nearly everyone. He was falsely accused of treason, whipped, tortured and executed. Jesus died a penniless, friendless, homeless, convicted felon.

Jesus knows what's it like to go through tough times. He knows what it's like to be hurt (physically, emotionally and psychologically) and to see your life unravel before your very eyes. No matter how bad the circumstances in your life are getting, Jesus can totally identify.

In fact, Jesus said that everyone who chooses to follow him will have a rough time in this life. He once told his followers,

All men will hate you because of me, but he who stands firm to the end will be saved. (Matthew 10:22 NIV)

When nothing's going right, stand firm. Stick with him. Let him know what you're going through. Jesus can understand and help you through whatever life throws your way. Don't give up on God. He won't ever give up on you.

from the gut

Okay, there's only one way to say this, God—life sucks.

It's past annoying me. It's past getting on my nerves. It's past not making sense. It just plain sucks. Nothing's going right. Nothing makes sense. Nothing at all. It's like someone just flushed all my dreams down the toilet.

Why does life have to be so rough?

I mean, maybe you've got your reasons and everything, but I don't get why you're slamming me right now. Even though I probably wouldn't admit this to anyone else but you, it hurts. I feel attacked and betrayed and let down and discouraged and sometimes I feel like just giving up on it all.

Is there something I'm missing here? Some reason why things are unraveling that I just haven't been informed of yet?

O Jesus, I know life doesn't revolve around me. It's just that right now I guess I've lost perspective. It's hard for me to see clearly. God, I know that even though my life isn't going the way I want it to, still you want me to stand firm.

Help me do that!

I can't make it on my own. I'll never make it on my own. Right now, more than ever, I need you . . .

"Teach us, good Lord, to give and not count the cost, to fight and not heed the wounds, to toil and not seek for rest, to labor and not ask for any reward, save that knowing that we do your will."

—st. ignatius of loyola (1491-1556), founder of the jesuit order

---

from the heart

okay God, here's what's going on in my life . . .

_____
_____
_____
_____

here are three things i wish you'd majorly change around . . .

1. _____
_____
_____

2. _____
_____
_____

3. _____
_____
_____

here's something i've always wanted to tell you but have never actually said . . .

_____
_____
_____
_____

God, remind me that you're in control whenever these things happen . . .

_____
_____
_____
_____

"Give all your worries and cares to God, for he cares about what happens to you."

1 Peter 5:7

JESUS knew what it was like to lose someone close. He was good friends with a man named Lazarus. When Lazarus died, Jesus knew he could bring him back to life. Jesus also knew he'd see Lazarus in Heaven someday. But still, when they took Jesus to the tomb, he burst into tears. He couldn't help it. The grief was too much for him. His humanity took over, and he wept.

And when the people who were there saw it, they were impressed by Jesus' love and compassion for Lazarus. The depth of Jesus' pain was clear to them.

When Jesus saw her weeping, and the Jews who had come along with her also weeping, he was deeply moved in spirit and troubled. "Where have you laid him?" he asked.
"Come and see, Lord," they replied.
Jesus wept.
Then the Jews said, "See how he loved him!" (John 11:33-36 NIV)

God never intended for us to lose our loved ones. God never intended for us to have to experience the awful tragedy of death. It's always been his plan to live in peace and harmony with his creation, side by side with his children.

But Adam and Eve chose to do their own thing rather than God's. And each of us has followed in their footsteps. The Bible calls it sin, and those stained with sin can't live forever in the presence of a perfect God. So, death has been stalking us ever since.

And even with the knowledge of God's power to save and the hope that comes from trusting in Christ, sometimes there's nothing to do but weep over death.

Just like Jesus did.

from the gut

God, they say you're the author of life—but all I can think about right now is death. They say you're the one who gives life and the one who takes it away. The giving part I can believe. But the taking part? How could you do that? If they're right, I guess you've got your reasons. But I don't get it!

Why? Why did you have to take away someone I care about so much? Do you even understand how much it hurts to love someone and then lose 'em? Why did you create a world so full of pain and sadness and loss?

I just wanna scream at someone, and I guess right now that's you. Why? Why? Why?!

I guess, to be honest, I wanna blame someone and I don't even know who to blame. Does it matter? Would blaming you make the pain less real?

God, help me make sense of this pain. That's all I really want. That's what I really need. Help me to think in a straight line again. Most of all, comfort me. Let me cry in front of you and not be ashamed. Just like Jesus did.

Help me, God. Help me . . .

"Death is no more than passing from one room into another. But there's a difference for me, you know. Because in that other room I shall be able to see."
—helen keller (1880-1968), inspirational deaf and blind overcomer

from the heart

when i think of death, all i can i think of is . . .

_____

_____

_____

_____

right now i need you to remind me that . . .

_____

_____

_____

_____

here's how i'm feeling right now . . .

_____

_____

_____

_____

God, here's what i need you to do for me . . .

_____

_____

_____

_____

deeper and further

Both Christians and non-Christians mourn when someone dies. Read 1 Thessalonians 4:13, 14. What's the difference between the way the two groups grieve? Why is this important to remember? What hope does this verse hold out for you as you consider your own mortality?

"God will shower us with his comfort through Christ."

2 Corinthians 1:5

JESUS lived side by side with his followers for three years. He camped with them, ate with them, laughed with them, hiked with them. And even after all that time of being so close to him, his closest friends and family still didn't really get it—who he was or what his life was really all about.

The religious leaders accused him of being a demon-possessed foreigner. His friends thought he was some kind of political rebel who was gonna lead them out of servitude to the Romans. There even came a day when his family members thought he was out of his mind.

If anyone ever felt misunderstood, it was Jesus.

One time, when Jesus warned his friends about the false teachings of the religious leaders, he compared their dangerous heresies to yeast. And once again, his disciples didn't really understand any of it. They thought Jesus was talking about what they were gonna eat for supper! That's when Jesus lost it. He just shook his head and said:

Won't you ever understand? Don't you remember the five thousand I fed with five loaves, and the baskets of food that were left over? Don't you remember the four thousand I fed with seven loaves, with baskets of food left over? How could you even think I was talking about food? (Matthew 16:9-11)

Jesus knew what it was like to be misunderstood. The only one who really understood Jesus was his true Father, his heavenly Father, God himself.

When you have a problem so deep that no one else seems to understand, you can be assured that the same God who listened to Jesus, understood Jesus and cared about Jesus, listens, understands and cares about you as well.

If anyone knows what you're going through, God does. If anyone can feel what you're feeling, if anyone can see things from your point of view, and provide real, lasting hope, it's God.

He's listening right now. What do you need to tell him?

from the gut

God, sometimes I don't know what to do. It's like no one understands where I'm coming from. My parents are completely clueless. My friends don't get what I'm trying to say. And the more I try to make everyone understand me, the more lost and alone I feel. What am I supposed to do?

I do my best to make sure I'm being clear, but it doesn't always work. People get hurt, they misunderstand me, they turn the things I say and do all around to mean something I never intended. And usually it's the people I care about the most who misunderstand me the most. Why is that?

But God, you understand me, don't you? You can see where I'm really hurting and how I'm really feeling deep inside and where I'm coming from, can't you?

I'm screaming inside my soul! No one sees me. No one understands. So what should I do, God? Are you really there; do you really care?

Jesus, you must know at least a little bit how I feel. I mean, toward the end of your life hardly anyone listened to you anymore. And sometimes you got tired of having to repeat and explain yourself. They just didn't get it, did they?

God, it helps just to know that you're listening. Even if no one else understands me, I'm glad there's at least one place I can go where I won't be misunderstood at all—in your arms. That's where I wanna go, and stay, right now . . .

> "One may have a blazing hearth in one's soul and yet no one ever comes to sit by it. Passers-by see only a wisp of smoke rising from the chimney and continue on their way."
>
> —vincent van gogh (1853-1890), artist

from the heart

more than anything else, here's what i wish people understood about me . . .

_____
_____
_____
_____

people think i'm . . . _____

_____
_____
_____
_____

. . . but i'm really . . . _____

_____
_____
_____
_____

here's one of the things about myself i've always been afraid to tell people . . .

_____
_____
_____
_____
_____

Why do we want to be understood so badly? People are so complex, intricate and unique, can you ever really hope to understand someone else? Why or why not? Read John 2:25 and Colossians 2:3. How does it change how you feel about God to realize he's the only one who can ever really, truly, understand you?

"O Lord, you have examined my heart and know everything about me."

Psalm 139:1

I SEE people walking past me and in my soul I wanna scream, "Do you even see me? Do I even matter to you?" But I'm silent and so are they and they just walk on by. I stand there in their wake like a rock in a river. Everyone floats past me. No one notices me. They just slide on by in the current of life.

O Jesus, I know what it feels like to be alone. I know what it feels like to look into the eyes of other people and see that I don't matter to them at all!

I'm so lonely, God. We have so much technology in our world, and science and freedom, but we have so little real relationship and friendship. And love.

I need you! Now, more than ever. I know you tasted loneliness. You tasted it on the cross, more deeply than I've ever tasted it. Than anyone has.

God, part of me knows you're there. Part of me knows you've promised never to leave me. But I don't feel you. I know about you, but just knowing isn't enough for me right now. I need to feel—in my heart, not just in my head—that you're here. Because right now it seems like everyone else has left me, too.

Jesus, didn't you say that God would never leave us? Doesn't the Bible say nothing can separate us from your love? Then why do I feel so separated? Why do I feel so alone?

Jesus, did you really cry out, "My God! My God! Why have you forsaken me?" Did you really know what it's like to feel like God is no longer there?

You did! I know you did! And I know you know how I feel right now.

Remind me that I'm never alone. Remind me in my heart where I need to hear it the most . . .

from the heart

when i feel lonely i feel like . . .

_____

_____

_____

_____

when i catch myself thinking too much about myself, i'll remind
myself that . . .

_____

_____

_____

_____

these are the times i feel the most lonely . . .

_____

_____

_____

_____

deeper and further

No one ever felt lonelier than Jesus did. Read Matthew 27:46.
Why can it be said that Jesus experienced the ultimate loneliness?
Do you think he understands what you're going through? How can
he help you when you feel lonely?

"God loves you dearly, and he has called you to be his very own people."
Romans 1:7

> "FOR we are God's masterpiece. He has created us anew in Christ Jesus, so that we can do the good things he planned for us long ago."
>
> Ephesians 2:10

from the gut

Shattered. That's how I feel. All broken apart inside.

I thought you were supposed to shape my life into a masterpiece? Well, my life doesn't feel like a masterpiece. It seems like a piece of broken pottery instead. Empty and shattered. Pieces of my dreams lay all around me. Sharp and wet and splintered and glistening in the sun.

There's a field of pain inside me stretching to the edge of the sky.

Where are you when I need you?

Where are you when I'm hurting?

And what am I supposed to do now? It's like you gave me all these hints that you cared about my dreams, and now I don't even know where to turn or what to believe in!

What gives!?

Could it be . . .

Could it be that you're already all around me? Could it be that you're the ground that lies before me? Could it be that you're the place my dreams have landed? Did you shatter my hopes, God, so that you could lay hold of them and reshape them like a potter does with his clay?

If that's true, then reshape me! Re-form me! Make me into the kind of person you want me to be. Remold my dreams. Help me to remember that my life is in your hands. You do more for me than I could ever do on my own.

God, help me to trust more in your plan than I do in my own circumstances.

Help me trust in your promises through all this pain. And help me remember that your plan for my life is bigger than any of my dreams could ever be . . .

> "May you get everything you wish for."
>
> —an eskimo curse

from the heart

these are the dreams i've had that now seem gone forever . . .

_____

_____

_____

_____

_____

deep in my heart i feel you calling me to a new dream; here it is . . .

_____

_____

_____

_____

_____

here's the first step i sense you asking me take in the direction of my new dream . . .

_____

_____

_____

_____

_____

> "You belong to Him [Jesus]. Tell him: 'I am yours—and if you cut me to pieces, every single piece will be only yours.'"
>
> —mother teresa (1910-1997), winner of the 1979 nobel peace prize

deeper and further

When Jesus first called him, Peter had no idea he'd end up preaching a sermon that would convert 3000 people in a single day. But that's exactly what happened (see Acts 2:41, 42). Once you buy into God's calling for your life, there's no telling where you'll end up or what he'll accomplish through you.

"What you ought to say is, 'If the Lord wants us to, we will live and do this or that.' Otherwise you will be boasting about your own plans, and all such boasting is evil."

James 4:15, 16

DURING the last week of his life, Jesus looked at the city of Jerusalem and wept—not for himself, but for them. Because they'd rejected him and would have to face the consequences of their choice. He didn't pretend the pain wasn't real, or that everything was okay. He saw the city and he wept.

Then, when Jesus arrived at the Garden of Gethsemane and knew he was about to be betrayed and handed over to be killed, he pulled a couple of his closest friends aside and told them,

My soul is overwhelmed with sorrow to the point of death. Stay here and keep watch with me. (Matthew 26:38 NIV)

Well, if you know the story, you know his friends fell asleep and Jesus felt more alone than ever.

Sadness strikes everyone. Sometimes it overwhelms us just like it overwhelmed Jesus. Hundreds of years before Jesus was even born, the prophet Isaiah wrote this about him:

He was despised and rejected by men, a man of sorrows, and familiar with suffering. Like one from whom men hide their faces he was despised. (Isaiah 53:3 NIV)

During the last days of Jesus' life, Isaiah's predictions came true down to the last letter. Despised. Rejected. Familiar with suffering. Jesus truly was a man of sorrows. On the cross he experienced the deepest rejection, the harshest suffering, the strongest grief, the darkest moods, the greatest sadness and the most unspeakable sins the world has ever known.

Why would Jesus be called a man of sorrows? Why would his soul be overwhelmed with so much sadness that he was at the point of death?

Because Jesus experienced all that human life has to offer. He looked at people so closely that he could see what they were like inside and out. He could see all the deep wounds and the old scars and the hidden tears. And not only did he see them, he experienced the pain along with them. And he still understands and experiences the pain today, along with us, too.

When you're sad, go to Jesus. He understands. And he has the power to help.

from the gut

God, sometimes it seems like it doesn't just rain outside, but it rains inside—in my heart, that is. It seems like there are raindrops the size of the world that swallow all my happiness and splatter down into the bottom of my soul. I feel like I'm drowning in sadness!

And it's this strange, suffocating kind of sadness that goes way beyond feeling disappointed or unhappy or depressed. It's a sadness so deep and so dark that it takes over my whole heart and surrounds my soul with sorrow and despair.

God, I know I'm not the only person to ever be this sad, but still, it feels like I am!

"If my sadness could be weighed and my troubles be put on the scales, they would be heavier than all the sands of the sea." (Job 6:2)

I can identify with the guy who wrote those words. Some of the stuff that really gets me down is stuff that might seem stupid to someone else. But it isn't stupid. Not to me. It's important. And it sometimes seems like there's nothing to do but cry. But I don't want to cry. Because, then people would know. Everyone would know.

Do you understand how I feel? Did you ever feel this sad? I guess you probably did. I mean, I guess you do feel this sad. At least sometimes.

Take my sadness away! Give me joy again!

Give me the strength and the hope and the faith to look past all the things that are dragging me down. Let me see that, with you, there's always something to look forward to. Something to believe in. Something that'll make all this suffering seem not so bad after all. I don't know what it'll take, Jesus. But I know I can't make it on my own. I need you now. I need your help . . .

"However long the night, the dawn will break."

from the heart

here's the biggest burden i'm carrying . . .

_____
_____
_____
_____
_____
_____

here's what i wish would happen when i feel this way . . .

_____
_____
_____
_____
_____
_____

here's what i think would help me the most right now . . .

_____
_____
_____
_____
_____
_____

Even God gets sad (Ephesians 4:30 says that God's Spirit grieves). The secret to becoming more like Jesus is finding joy in the Lord and taking our sorrow to him for healing. What does Nehemiah 8:10 say is the source of our strength? How does that make you feel?

Hope can help when you feel sad. Read Romans 15:13 and ask others to pray that verse for you when you feel sad.

"You keep track of all my sorrows. You have collected all my tears in your bottle. You have recorded each one in your book."

Psalm 56:8

WHEN Judas approached Jesus in the Garden of Gethsemane, he had it all figured out. He'd greet Jesus by giving him a friendly kiss on the cheek (kinda like a handshake today) and then the soldiers would arrest Jesus and Judas would get to keep his 30 pieces of silver.

And things went pretty much according to plan. Except that after Jesus was arrested, Judas began to have second thoughts about the whole thing. He realized that Jesus hadn't done anything wrong after all and that he'd turned over an innocent man to be killed.

So, Judas tried to undo the events he'd set into motion. He tried to return the money, but that didn't work. He tried to apologize, but the religious leaders just laughed at him. He felt guilty and sorry and desperate and alone. So finally, filled with grief and despair, Judas took his own life. He couldn't stand the thought of living with the guilt and knowledge of what he'd done.

Some people kill themselves because of guilt, like Judas did. Others end their lives because of hopelessness or loneliness or because they feel like failures. Many teens commit suicide out of a sense of anger at themselves or their families. Some even do it because of boredom or disappointment or revenge. Teens have killed themselves because of getting cut from athletic teams, receiving an unusually poor grade, breaking up with a boyfriend or having an argument with someone close to them.

But nearly always, the root causes of suicide are hopelessness, depression and despair.

Suicide is not a peaceful release from life or a romantic escape from suffering into eternal bliss. It is death. It ends a life prematurely and leaves behind a lot of pain for families and friends for years to come.

Forgiveness, not suicide, is God's solution to despair.

If you notice that you're thinking more and more about suicide, seek help and guidance from your youth leader, school counselor, teacher, coach or parent. Most communities have suicide help or prevention hotlines. Check your phone book, or call your local hospital, counseling center or a pastor at your church. Don't put it off! Talk to someone before you feel desperate or hopeless. If you are thinking about how and when to kill yourself or are pretty sure that you are ready to hurt yourself, call 911 for immediate help.

from the gut

Okay, God, here's the thing. I've thought about, I mean, I've really thought about it and I feel like ending my life. Ending everything. Killing myself. It seems like life doesn't really matter anymore. It's not that I think I'd be better off dead, it's more like I don't even care anymore about living.

And I gotta be honest, God. Those thoughts scare me. I'm scared of thinking these things and even more scared of actually doing them. Because I don't wanna do it. Not really. It's just that sometimes I feel so lonely or hurt or sad or angry that suicide seems like the only reasonable option.

In my head I know your answer to sadness and loneliness isn't suicide. It's the kind of solution that doesn't solve anything. But I don't know where to turn or who to talk to!

Help me, God! Don't leave me hanging! Show me the reality of a life that calls out to be lived! Pull me past these pits of darkness that I feel drawn into. And show me how to make it through these terrible times with your help!

Cut the cords of hopelessness and fill me with yourself instead . . .

from the heart

here's why i've been thinking so much about suicide lately . . .

_____

_____

_____

_____

_____

_____

when i feel like ending it all, i'll talk to . . .

_____

_____

_____

_____

_____

_____

when i feel lonely or hurt i'll try to do this stuff . . .

_____

_____

_____

_____

. . . instead of this stuff . . .

_____

_____

_____

_____

Read Zephaniah 3:17. How does this verse put your life into perspective? Did you even know that God felt this way about you? How does knowing God's view of your life change how you look at yourself? How does it affect what you're going through right now?

"Don't be afraid, for I am with you. Do not be dismayed, for I am your God. I will strengthen you. I will help you. I will uphold you with my victorious right hand. . . . I am holding you by your right hand—I, the LORD your God. And I say to you, 'Do not be afraid. I am here to help you.'"

Isaiah 41:10, 13

THERE were three strikes against her. First, she was a woman. And in Jesus' day, even though in God's eyes both men and women were equally valued, it wasn't that way with the religious leaders. All throughout society, women didn't have equal rights. They were pretty much second-class citizens.

Second, she was a Samaritan. Jews looked down on the people of Samaria because long ago they'd been Jews themselves. But over the years they'd intermingled and intermarried with the people of the neighboring lands. So, the Jews looked at them as half-breeds who were equal in their eyes to the mangy dogs that roamed the streets of Israel rooting through the garbage. Eek.

Finally, she was living a lifestyle that neither the Jews nor the Samaritans (nor God) approved of. She'd moved in with a guy she wasn't married to. And this happened only after a long string of divorces and ruined relationships.

Soon a Samaritan woman came to draw water, and Jesus said to her, "Please give me a drink." He was alone at the time because his disciples had gone into the village to buy some food.

The woman was surprised, for Jews refuse to have anything to do with Samaritans. She said to Jesus, "You are a Jew, and I am a Samaritan woman. Why are you asking me for a drink?"
(John 4:7-9)

You can understand her surprise when Jesus stopped to talk with her. And when he turned the conversation toward spiritual matters and her lifestyle choices, you can see why she tried to play the race card and attempted to shift the topic to nationalistic prejudice.

But in the end, the woman at the well was transformed by Jesus' acceptance, prophetic abilities and stirring words. She believed he really was the promised Savior and when she began her relationship with Jesus, the opinions of others began to matter less and less to her as the acceptance of Jesus took over her life.

And the same thing can happen to you.

from the gut

God, I guess it's different for everyone. Some people get looked down on because of their skin color or hair color or religion or age or interests or because they're a guy or a girl. For me it's because I'm

_____ *.*

I hate this whole deal with prejudice because most of the time people look down on you for stuff you can't even change. I guess it doesn't matter how smart or cute or athletic I am, there'll always be someone smarter or cuter or whatever. And there'll always be people who are quick to look down on me.

I guess I've never really thought of it before, but people looked down on you, too, didn't they? They mocked you because they didn't know who your real Dad was and they thought your mom was sleeping around and that you were an illegitimate child.

So, you know how words can sting, don't you?

Jesus, you helped that woman at the well to find her acceptance not in how she looked or where she came from or what she did, but through her faith in you. That's what I need. You did it for her. Do it for me. Let the opinions of others mean less and less to me as I walk closer and closer to you. And help wash away all the lingering pains of being looked down on, made fun of and mocked. That's the kind of healing I need. That's the kind of healing your Spirit gives.

Here I am. Help me where I need it the most . . .

"Fame is a vapor, popularity is an accident, money takes wings. Those who cheer you today may curse you tomorrow. The only thing that endures is character."
—o. j. simpson, 1968 heisman trophy winner and professional football star who was acquitted of murder charges

from the heart

i hate it when people look down on me because of my . . .

_____

_____

_____

_____

_____

_____

i admit that i sometimes look down on people who are . . .

_____

_____

_____

_____

_____

_____

deeper and further

How did Jesus respond to insults and injustice? Look up Luke 23:33, 34 to find out. Would you say that Jesus put Matthew 5:44 into practice? Why or why not? How does that affect your attitude concerning injustices?

"My dear brothers and sisters, how can you claim that you have faith in our glorious Lord Jesus Christ if you favor some people more than others?"

James 2:1

GOD, sometimes I feel like no matter where I go—school, ball games, the mall—that everyone else has all these really close friends and I'm left out of everything. Like no one notices me. Or cares about me.

And it hurts.

I know in my head that people care. People like my parents and teachers and my friends. But I don't always feel like they do. It's hard to explain, but I wish I felt more cared about. I wish people treated me like I really mattered.

When I was a kid I thought it'd be cool to be invisible. To go anywhere and do anything and never get caught. Never be seen.

But I had no idea I'd grow up to feel invisible. To slip through the cracks and land here, by myself, alone. Under a crumpled pile of my own hopes and dreams. I don't think anyone would even care if I were swept away into oblivion. No one would even notice.

Would you, God? Would you notice that I was missing? Would you care that I was gone?

Is it really true that you love me as a friend? And as a child? That you care about my hopes and dreams and my lonely, lonely days? Can you understand how I feel? I bet you can. I bet you sometimes feel like no one cares about you, too.

Help me, Jesus! Help me to remember that I do matter, to you. Help me to know your love in my head and my heart. Take this loneliness away and replace it with your presence. Thanks for listening . . .

And thanks, God, that I don't have to put on a show or act stupid to get you to notice me. Thanks, God, that I'm free to be wholly myself. At least with you.

> "If I am a legend, then why am I so lonely?"
> —judy garland (1922-1969), world-famous actress and entertainer

from the heart

here's what i wish everyone knew about me . . .

_____

_____

_____

_____

these are the times i feel most overlooked and invisible . . .

_____

_____

_____

_____

here's someone else i know who's invisible . . .

_____

deeper and further

Our reputation is what people think of us, our character is what we're really like. We only have control over one of those. Which one is it? Yet which one are we usually more concerned about? Why is that? What change needs to happen in your heart to switch it around? Read Proverbs 29:25 for help doing just that.

"God the Father chose you long ago, and the Spirit has made you holy."

1 Peter 1:2

WHEN the rooster crowed, Peter knew he'd blown it big time. He'd had three chances to stand up for Jesus and each time he'd failed to do so.

Now, you gotta picture this. Just a few hours earlier, Jesus warned him this was gonna happen, but Peter was like, "No way, Jesus! I'll stick with you to the end. I'd even die for you!" But Jesus just shook his head. "Peter, before daybreak you'll deny knowing me three times."

So, after Jesus was arrested, that's exactly what happened. When the people standing around the courtyard saw Peter, they recognized him. And three times in a row he just flat out denied even knowing who Jesus was.

Maybe he was intimidated. Or embarrassed. Or afraid of what might happen to him. But whatever his reasons were, he did precisely what Jesus had predicted he'd do. And then, as they were leading Jesus away, Peter looked up and saw Jesus. At the moment of Peter's greatest weakness, Jesus looked into his friend's eyes.

At that moment the Lord turned and looked at Peter. Then Peter remembered that the Lord had said, "Before the rooster crows tomorrow morning, you will deny me three times." And Peter left the courtyard, crying bitterly. (Luke 22:61, 62)

There was probably love in Jesus' eyes. And forgiveness. And acceptance. But remember that Jesus was totally human. So there had to be at least a little pain, too.

Any way you cut it, Peter hurt Jesus. And Peter knew it. That's why he wept bitterly.

But in the end, Jesus forgave Peter. And eventually their friendship became stronger and deeper than ever. And one day, Peter did exactly what he'd said he would do, he ended up dying for the man he denied knowing that night when the rooster crowed.

from the gut

God, I did it again.

How come I can't control myself? How come I always end up saying the kind of stuff and doing the kind of stuff that leaves such deep wounds in the lives of the people I care so much about?

When I hurt someone like this, I usually find some good-sounding excuses—"she deserved it" . . . "he's taking it out of context" . . . "I was just having a bad day" . . . "she misunderstood me" . . . "I've been stressed out, so it's not really my fault" . . . "I didn't mean it" . . . "he's making a big deal out of nothing" . . .

But the fact is—it was a big deal. And it was my fault. And I can't seem to stop on my own . . . boy, this is hard to do . . . okay, here goes . . . I admit it. . . . All the pain was my fault. All the wounds are my doing.

God, I don't even know where to start in making this right, but give me the guts to at least try. Give me the courage to do what I'm afraid to do. Help me to say, "I'm sorry," and mean it from the real place in my heart.

And then, even if my apology isn't accepted, help me to still call 'em my friend.

God, I also wanna ask that you help the person I've hurt to recover. Turn this thing around somehow. In your mysterious way, bring a blessing out of this disaster. Thanks for listening. Thanks for being there . . .

"My deepest apologies to those who were offended, affected, or hurt by this insanely twisted deformation of my words and intent."

—johnny depp, movie actor

from the heart

here's the name of the person i hurt:

_____

here's what i did . . .

_____

_____

_____

here's how i'd like to see things change between us . . .

_____

_____

_____

here's what i feel you want me to do to make things right . . .

_____

_____

_____

deeper and further

Sometimes it takes a long time to make things right between friends after one of them has been hurt. Sometimes things are never the same again. Look up Proverbs 27:6. Does this verse surprise you? Why or why not? What can you learn from this verse that applies to your life right now?

Now read Philippians 4:2, 3. What was going on in the church? What was Paul's advice? How does that apply to your life today?

"Confess your sins to each other and pray for each other so that you may be healed."

James 5:16

prayers
of
doubt

JESUS knew there'd be times when we would be tempted to give up on prayer because we just weren't seeing the kind of results we'd hoped for or expected.

That's why he told a story about a lady who kept taking her case to the court of a certain judge so that she could finally get justice. The only problem was that this judge didn't care about justice and wouldn't listen to her case. He was crooked. So the lady kept coming back again and again and again. And he kept refusing until she wore him out. He just wanted to get her off his back, so he finally granted her request.

But to Jesus, this story goes deeper than just a lady and a two-bit judge. Jesus *compares* the widow in the story to us when we go to God in prayer. And he *contrasts* the judge in the story to God.

Learn a lesson from this evil judge. Even he rendered a just decision in the end, so don't you think God will surely give justice to his chosen people who plead with him day and night? Will he keep putting them off? I tell you, he will grant justice to them quickly! (Luke 18:6-8)

You see, if even the crooked judge gave the woman justice, how much more will our holy God, who is totally fair and just, give us what we ask for? And he's not gonna wait around. He's gonna listen and respond. As Jesus put it another time:

If you sinful people know how to give good gifts to your children, how much more will your heavenly Father give good gifts to those who ask him. (Matthew 7:11)

Don't give up. Keep bringing your requests to God no matter what. Even when there isn't any answer. *Especially* when there isn't any answer. Even when you've been coming for a long time and there's no answer and it seems like God isn't listening. He is.

God guarantees that when we ask for something with a believing heart, he'll either give us precisely what we ask for, or something even better for our lives and our relationships with him.

Okay. It's time I told you how I feel about this whole prayer thing. It stinks. I ask you for guidance and I just end up feeling like I'm stumbling around in the dark. I ask you for help and nothing happens. I ask you for answers and all you give me is silence.

What's the deal? Don't you care about me? What kind of conversation is this? What kind of a relationship is it where one person does all the talking? You promised to hear me and answer me. What gives? If I didn't know any better I'd say all this silence either proves you're not there or that you don't really care about what happens to me.

Because you're embarrassing the faith I have in you.

Silence. Still silence. Even when I complain to you. What does it mean? Where are you God, when I need you most? You never seem to answer me. Do you even care about me at all? Why are you being so silent when you know my heart and you see how important this is to me?

> "When I was crossing into Gaza I was asked at the check post whether I was carrying any weapons. I replied: Oh yes, my prayer books."
> —mother teresa (1910-1997), winner of the 1979 nobel peace prize

from the heart

here are the prayers i just don't seem to hear answers to . . .

_____

_____

_____

here's why i think you're not answering me . . .

_____

_____

_____

here's what i'll do when you don't seem to be listening . . .

_____

_____

_____

deeper and further

Job kept asking God for justice. In chapter after chapter, the book of Job records his pleadings and prayers to God. Until finally, when God does speak to him, Job is stunned and humbled into silence. Read about it in Job 40:3-5. Why do you think Job was so humbled? What insight does that give into your life today?

"Then Jesus told his disciples a parable to show them that they should always pray and not give up."

Luke 18:1 NIV

SOLOMON tried to figure it all out. He thought maybe he could decipher the secrets of life, see the patterns and make sense of it all. So, he sought out wisdom everywhere while reflecting about life. In the book of Ecclesiastes he observed that:

- the more we try to figure out life, the more confused and mixed up we get (chapter 1:18)
- filling our lives with stuff only provides more distraction, not more fulfillment (chapter 2)
- no matter how smart or stupid we are, we all die and are soon forgotten and that seems completely senseless (2:16)
- we work hard hoping for happiness and then we die and all the stuff we've accumulated goes to someone else who didn't work for it at all (2:21, 22)
- life is filled with terrible suffering and tragedy and those in power take advantage of the poor and helpless (4:1-3)
- money doesn't bring happiness, it only brings more and more headaches (5:10-12)
- health and wealth don't always go together and that's a tragic injustice (6:1, 2)
- no one knows the future, so make the most of today and stop worrying, fretting, scheming and striving to get ahead so much (6:10-12; 10:14)
- despite our best laid plans and intentions, nothing is certain in life except for death (7:14; 9:12)
- life isn't fair or just or kind, so we shouldn't be surprised by injustice, suffering or pain (8:14)
- everything in life has risks (10:8, 9)
- you'll never figure out God's ways, they're too mysterious (11:5)
- age doesn't matter much in the long run since we all face a meaningless death at the end anyhow (11:8-10)

Solomon concluded that there's no secret formula to life. As hard as we try to, we'll never figure out all its twists and turns and seeming injustices. It didn't make sense to Solomon, the world's wisest man. And it's not always gonna make sense to us, either.

from the gut

God, I don't understand my life. I look around and I see so much injustice and suffering and pain. People who don't deserve it are getting honored while the people who deserve honor are getting despised and put down and forgotten.

Life isn't fair. It's so full of meaningless pain and suffering. Those who can, take advantage of those who can't fight back.

Every day I have less of my life before me. Every hour I leave more of my life trailing behind me in the dust, rippling backward into the pages of time.

Every breath I take, every moment my heart beats, my past grows and my future shrinks.

And yet, I plan as if I'll still be here tomorrow. I live as if I'll never die. Does that make any sense? Why is it so hard to admit we're mortal? And that life is so fragile?

As hard as I try to change things—in others and in myself—they stay pretty much the same. Or at least they don't change for long. Good people die young while bitter, angry, resentful people seem to live forever! Where's the justice in that? When I do my best, I sometimes still fail while others who cheat and lie and pull strings get ahead. And even though I tell myself that it's better to do what's right than what's wrong, and that it's better to pursue wisdom rather than a life of stupidity . . . I'm not always convinced that that's true. Because we all die anyway, so what does it really matter in the end how we act?

I know this, too—life is a mystery and death is a tragedy and hope only comes to us as a gift from you.

So, help me to find meaning in my relationship with you rather than seeking it in the mysteries of life in this mixed-up world . . .

> "Education never ends, Watson. It is a series of lessons with the greatest for the last."
>
> —sherlock holmes, legendary detective

from the heart

when life doesn't make sense, help me to remember these things about you . . .

_____

_____

_____

_____

_____

here are my three biggest questions about life . . .

1. _____

_____

_____

2. _____

_____

_____

3. _____

_____

_____

here's something i really don't understand about the way my life is going right now . . .

_____

_____

_____

_____

_____

deeper and further

God never minds our questions as long as we don't think we know better than he does. Read Romans 9:20-22. What's your attitude when it comes to questioning God? If you could ask God one question, what would it be? If you could take back one question, what would it be?

"Oh, what a wonderful God we have! How great are his riches and wisdom and knowledge! How impossible it is for us to understand his decisions and his methods! For who can know what the Lord is thinking? Who knows enough to be his counselor?"

Romans 11:33, 34

fall on me like snow

O GOD, I sense that you're there. I sense you not with my physical eyes, but with my spiritual senses.

And yet, there seems to be this distance between us. And I don't know if I've caused the rift by my selfishness and sin and envy of others, or maybe by my past mistakes or my guilt and regrets. But for whatever reason, you seem far away. And right now I need you close by.

O Lord, I need you close by!

I'm reaching out to you the best I know how and you're still out of reach, so reach out to me, Father!

Take my hand and touch my heart. Spread your Spirit over my wounds and heal me from the lingering injuries of my past mistakes. O Lord, cover my life like snow. The winter landscape of my soul is vast and frozen. Cover me with yourself like a glistening blanket. Cover me with your purity and your holiness. The land cannot rise up to greet the snow, and I cannot rise up to greet you because my selfish, sinful tendencies hold me down. So fall upon me, O God! I can receive you. I can welcome you. That I can do. That much I will do!

I greet the snowflakes of your grace as they land upon my soul . . .

remind me of your grace

Remind me that my longing for you itself is evidence of your presence. My desire for your intimacy is a clue to your work within my soul.

Wherever my life leads me, remind me that you're already there waiting for me.

However abandoned I may feel, remind me that you'll never, ever leave me.

Though I may try to run from you, don't let me go far without allowing something in my soul to wake me up once again to my lostness and your searching Spirit.

Despite the hatred in the world, remind me that nothing can separate me from your love.

However desperately I may seek you, remind me that you sought me first. And I can only find you when I find myself in the center of your love.

And remind me that however lost I feel sometimes, I'm still on a journey. You are the path beneath my feet, the sun that lights my way, the companion by my side and the final destination that I seek.

Remind me that it's not the depth of my longing that brings you close, but the length of your grace extended down toward my heart . . .

bridge the gap between us

God, sometimes I feel this yawning gap between us. At first I thought it was caused by you. I thought maybe it was because you didn't understand me, or reach out to me or offer yourself to me despite my imperfections. But the more I learn about you, the more I realize that I was the one who didn't understand you, or reach out to you or offer myself to you. And it was my imperfections themselves (the ones I so quickly excuse and rationalize), that caused the deep rift between you and me.

And I say, "O God, look at that great canyon stretching before me!"

And you smile and set your hand on my shoulder and say, "What canyon? The rift is gone. The gulf is crossed. There isn't anything between us at all."

And so I fall to my knees and worship you for saving me from myself . . .

"Thanks be to you, our Lord Jesus Christ, for all the benefits that you have given, for all the pains and insults that you have borne for us. Most merciful Redeemer, Friend, and Brother, may we know you more clearly, love you more dearly, and follow you more nearly, day by day."

—richard of chichester (1197-1253), bishop and barefoot preacher

from the heart

here's how i know you're reaching out to me . . .

_____

_____

_____

_____

_____

_____

here's how i know you're still there for me . . .

_____

_____

_____

_____

_____

_____

here's something i've let get between us . . .

_____

_____

_____

_____

_____

_____

Why do you think God doesn't make himself more visible? What purpose do you think that serves? If God is always everywhere, why do you think he seems more distant at certain times? Read Jeremiah 29:11 and think about the presence, plan and purposes of God, especially when he seems distant or silent to the cries of your heart.

"I go east, but he is not there. I go west, but I cannot find him. I do not see him in the north, for he is hidden. I turn to the south, but I cannot find him. But he knows where I am going. And when he has tested me like gold in a fire, he will pronounce me innocent."

Job 23:8-10

FOR awhile now I've believed in you, God. It hasn't been all that hard. It's sort of been natural and expected in our culture.

But now, well . . . how can I say this . . . I've started to question some things. Like how come there's so much pain the world if you have so much love? And how come you're not more visible and active in the world? And how come those who claim to believe in you sometimes act worse than your enemies?

I want proof of your existence. You don't seem real anymore, and I don't know what to believe. I wonder if you're even listening to me. You seem so distant. My doubts are crowding out my beliefs.

Maybe I've lost my faith in you. Or maybe, just maybe, I'm finally finding out that there's more to faith than just believing what you're told. Maybe faith also has to do with believing the truth even when the evidence seems to disprove it. Maybe faith is believing despite what you see, not because of it.

I don't know. But I do know a couple things—life is more confusing than I ever thought it would be. And believing in you isn't as simple as I first thought it would be.

But that's okay. I guess. As long as I'm struggling with it I guess that's a good sign.

I want to believe in you more. Give me more faith, God. Show me what I need to see to keep believing in you . . .

> "Faith is to believe what we do not see, and the reward of faith is to see what we believe."
>
> —saint augustine (354-430), bishop of hippo, defender of the christian faith

from the heart

these things cause me to doubt you . . .

_____

_____

_____

the next time i doubt you, i'll do this . . .

_____

_____

_____

here's my definition of faith . . .

_____

_____

_____

deeper and further

If you've been walking with Jesus for a while, you know that difficult times will come. Read John 10:27-30. What reassurances does Jesus give in these verses? Who's more powerful than anyone? What assurance does that give you when you feel like you're slipping from his grip?

"'My Lord and my God!' Thomas exclaimed. Then Jesus told him, 'You believe because you have seen me. Blessed are those who haven't seen me and believe anyway.'"

John 20:28, 29

THE LORD said, "Go out and stand on the mountain in the presence of the LORD, for the LORD is about to pass by."

Then a great and powerful wind tore the mountains apart and shattered the rocks before the LORD, but the LORD was not in the wind. After the wind there was an earthquake, but the LORD was not in the earthquake. After the earthquake came a fire, but the Lord was not in the fire. And after the fire came a gentle whisper.
(1 Kings 19:11, 12 NIV)

from the gut

Whisper to me, O God! Be a gentle voice in my ear!

Speak to my soul! I long to hear your words inside me. I need to know you're real. Because I can see the wind and the earthquake and the fire all too well. And I know you aren't in them. So speak to me, O God!

God, how come it's so hard to see you in the everyday moments that crowd my time? Why aren't you more present in the rush of traffic and the busy signals and the shopping lines and the failed tests? There are so many distractions and frustrations! Sometimes I long for a life so simple that I can't help but see you everywhere!

God, you're so freeing, yet the world is so visible. And it's easy to get caught up in the things I see rather than the spiritual realities I don't.

The things that I can see seem real. The things that I can taste and touch and feel seem real. But you, God, you don't seem real to me right now. It's like a fish remains unaware of the water, though he's immersed in it. And it affects all of how he sees and interprets the world. Are you that present? Are you really surrounding me, embracing me, immersing me, or is my faith all an illusion after all?

*Make your presence real to me. You are Spirit, so I couldn't expect
to see you with my eyes. Help me to sense you in my spirit. Confirm to
me that you are the true reality, more lasting than all that I see, more
real than the air I breathe and more solid than the earth beneath my
feet . . .*

> "As putting our hand near the flames and experiencing the warmth of the fire
> proves the existence of fire, so experiencing God in spirit is the only strong and solid
> proof of his existence."
> —sundar singh, (1889-1929) indian spiritual leader who converted to christianity
> when he was 16 years old

from the heart

here's why you don't seem real . . .

_____
_____
_____
_____

here's how i'd like you to confirm your presence in my life . . .

_____
_____
_____
_____

here's the biggest reason i believe in you even though i can't
prove it . . .

_____
_____
_____
_____

When the religious leaders pressed Jesus for proof of his claims he refused to give it (see Matthew 12:38-45). Why do you think that is? At least part of the reason was that Jesus wanted followers of faith, not logic. Our relationship with God isn't based on proof and knowledge, but trust and reliance. What are you leaning on? What needs to change in your relationship to him?

"So we don't look at the troubles we can see right now; rather, we look forward to what we have not yet seen. For the troubles we see will soon be over, but the joys to come will last forever."

2 Corinthians 4:18

> "Doubt is a pain too lonely to know that faith is his twin brother."
> —kahlil gibran (1883-1931), poet, philosopher and artist

JESUS, I've longed for you, I've learned of you, but I wonder if I've ever really believed in you. Oh, sure, I can recite all the right information about who you are and what you've done and why you came, but does that mean I believe it? What does it really mean to believe in you?

It's not the same as weighing the evidence and coming to a reasonable conclusion. Faith is more than an educated guess. And it's not just a guessing game or a safe bet or a good gamble. And it's not the same thing as looking for proof because then you don't have to believe anything at all. If you can prove something, there's no place for faith left.

God, you ask us to believe, which means there's space in there for doubt.

*Help me to believe, **really** believe in you. As much as I believe tomorrow will come, as much as I believe in the waves on the sea, as much as I believe the stars will glimmer in the sky tonight, as much as I believe I'll be alive to enjoy my next breath.*

*God, give me confidence that you **are** real and that my relationship with you is real and that your promises for my life **are** true. Now and forever . . .*

"You love him even though you have never seen him. Though you do not see him, you trust him; and even now you are happy with a glorious, inexpressible joy. Your reward for trusting him will be the salvation of your souls."

1 Peter 1:8, 9

> "The Christian life is not a constant high. I have my moments of deep discouragement. I have to go to God in prayer with tears in my eyes, and say, 'O God, forgive me,' or 'Help me.'"
>
> —billy graham, evangelist

here's why i sometimes doubt you're real . . .

_____

_____

here's how i think a true believer would respond to you . . .

_____

_____

here's what i need to do when i question my faith . . .

_____

_____

deeper and further

Belief and unbelief, trust and doubt can exist in the same place at the same time. Sometimes unbelief threads its way into belief, and doubt weaves its way into the fabric of your trust. So it's not always a question of which do you have, but which do you have more of. It isn't a matter of "one *or* the other," but "both one *and* the other."

Look up Mark 9:14-24. Based on these verses, would you say the father believed or doubted? Why do you say that? What reassurance for you is there in these verses? What prayer did the father in the story pray to Jesus that we can pray today in our times of doubt? Do you need to pray it right now?

"And when you believed in Christ, he identified you as his own by giving you the Holy Spirit, whom he promised long ago. The Spirit is God's guarantee that he will give us everything he promised and that he has purchased us to be his own people."

Ephesians 1:13, 14

> "If you look for me in earnest, you will find me when you seek me."
> —God (jeremiah 29:13)

PAUL stood before the leading rulers and philosophers of the world and told them about the God whom he had learned to love. After describing God's creative abilities, his power and supernatural existence, Paul said,

From one man he created all the nations throughout the whole earth. He decided beforehand which should rise and fall, and he determined their boundaries.

His purpose in all of this was that the nations should seek after God and perhaps feel their way toward him and find him—though he is not far from any one of us. (Acts 17:26, 27)

God's purpose in orchestrating all of creation, history, governments and empires was so that we would seek him. And find him. Though he is not far from any of us.

If you feel like something is missing from your life and you wonder if maybe something is wrong with you, there's nothing wrong. You were made to be dissatisfied with this life. God planted that dissatisfaction in your heart so that you would reach out for him. You were designed to search for God. He put those longings in your heart.

It may be that you've been searching in the wrong places for the fulfillment that only can come from finding and knowing God. It's like, if you're thirsty and you drink ocean water, it's never gonna satisfy you. It'll only add to your thirst. That's the way it is with the things of this world. Rather than relieve you, they deceive you. And even though they appear to promise to quench the thirst you have for satisfaction and fulfillment, only God can do that.

Jesus promised "water of life" to all who come to him. That means he wants to give eternal, ultimate refreshment for your soul. As Jesus once said, *"Come to me, all of you who are weary and carry heavy burdens, and I will give you rest" (Matthew 11:28).*

Right now. Come to him. He's waiting. And he's not far from any of us. He's not far from you.

diving deeper

I know you're there, God. I sense your presence, but also your distance. I need you closer. I need you here with me . . .

Are there any things in my life that are keeping me from you? If so, dig 'em up by the roots and pull 'em out completely. Are there doubts that I have that are distancing me from you? If so, erase 'em once and for all by the sweeping grace of your Spirit.

Are my fears causing rifts between us? If so, quiet the waters, calm my fears and still the striving nature of my soul. Maybe I'm really afraid to dive into the depths of knowing you so I sit here on shore trying to convince myself that I've really gone beneath the surface and been swept away in the currents of your grace. I've been afraid to even get wet. Not anymore. Take me deeper!

I see glimpses of you everywhere—in the glint of sunlight sparkling off a river . . . in the thousand shades of green painted in a forest . . . in the glimmer of distant starlight . . . in the echo of hope that I feel deep within my soul.

But God, I don't want to just glimpse you any longer. I want to see you fully! I want to stare into your eyes forever! I don't want to see you from a distance, but to feel you up close. I don't want you to lie on the outskirts, but at the very center of who I am. I'm searching, God, and I want to be found by your side . . .

let me lose myself in you

There's nothing I long for more than you. More than food or water or air I desire only to be close to you.

It's not an easy journey, this walk in your direction. It's required more faith than I ever imagined I'd need and more trust than I've ever been asked to give anyone.

But God, you're worth it! I will walk the journey! I will believe your promises! I will trust your Spirit!

When we search for you, we look everywhere only to find in the end of our journey that you'd been with us since the beginning. We're so intent on the search that we don't even notice your presence during the trip. Eternal Lord, open my eyes that I might see you beside me now, before the road passes beneath my feet!

I long to lose all my yearnings except those that drive me to your arms. Let me find my home and my Lord. Lead me on and let me be found in you!

"Never look down to test the ground before taking your next step; Only he who keeps his eye fixed on the far horizon will find his right road."
—dag hammarskjöld (1905-1961), united nations secretary-general, winner of the 1961 nobel peace prize

---

from the heart

God, here's my deepest longing . . .

_____

_____

_____

_____

_____

God, here's my deepest need . . .

_____

_____

_____

_____

_____

_____

deeper and further

Look up Romans 3:9-12. Why do you think it says no one seeks God? Jesus said all who seek will find (see Luke 11:9-13). Do these verses contradict each other? Why or why not? In verse 13 what does Jesus say about the Father giving the Holy Spirit? Have you done that? If not, what's holding you back?

"Oh, that we might know the Lord! Let us press on to know him! Then he will respond to us as surely as the arrival of dawn or the coming of rains in early spring."

Hosea 6:3

prayers
of
praise

PICTURE an old, run-down, deserted house. Can you see the doors hanging awkwardly on the hinges? The broken windows? The faded paint and neglected lawn? Inside, the wiring is sticking through the walls and the plumbing doesn't work.

If your parents bought a place like that, they'd probably remodel before moving in. They'd rewire, clean out the trash, repaint the walls, get the windows and pipes fixed. Then, finally, you could all move in and make it your new home.

Jesus does just the opposite.

When he finds a life that's falling apart, or a heart in need of repair, he moves in first and then remodels from the inside out. You don't have to change first or clean up your life. He accepts people "as is."

That's why he hung around with the kind of people the religious leaders looked down on—prostitutes, thieves, crooked businessmen, the "scum of society."

When they complained about this, Jesus replied:

Healthy people don't need a doctor—sick people do. I have come to call sinners to turn from their sins, not to spend my time with those who think they are already good enough. (Luke 5:31, 32)

Jesus came looking for those in need of spiritual healing, not the best-looking homes on the block, but the worst. And when he changes you, in big ways and small, you can feel his miracle-working carpentry in your soul.

It's a good thing Jesus doesn't require us to meet a certain standard before he's willing to accept us, move into our lives and take up residence in our hearts. If he did, we'd all be in trouble.

It doesn't matter what you've done or how run-down your life is, once you invite him to stay, Jesus moves in. He accepts you the way you are. Then, once he's inside, he starts the housecleaning and the remodeling process for you.

Talk about home improvement!

from the gut

Glory.

I know very little of glory. Not many things are glorious. I've glimpsed the edges of glory in the mountain mists, the auburn sky, the twilight of winter and the sunlight trapped inside an iceberg. But I've never seen glory in anything that we humans have made. We call it "progress" when we make stuff. We call our inventions "breakthroughs."

But all I see are straight lines and architecture and sidewalks and form and function, but not glory. When you create stuff, God, you weave miracles into it. You've even woven miracles into the fabric of my life.

The greatest miracle of all is the miracle of faith. It's amazing how you choose us and use us to work your will in the world.

Jesus, some miracles are big and noticeable. Like the ones you did—walking on the water, feeding 5000 people with a little boy's sack lunch, raising dead people back to life, calming a raging hurricane. It's hard to miss miracles like that.

But some miracles are smaller and go unnoticed—the miracle of a heartbeat . . . the miraculous mixture of oxygen in the air . . . the moment when faith is born in an unbelieving soul . . . we're so used to miracles that we overlook 'em or feel comfortable naming them— gravity, imagination, dawn, laughter, rainbows, healing, chrysalis, photosynthesis.

Something as common as light itself is a mystery to scientists who still can't decide if it acts more like a particle or a wave. Just because a miracle happens every day doesn't make it less of a miracle.

And now your miracles have touched my life! You've made my life glorious, O God. For that I thank you and bow before you . . .

> "Everything is a miracle. It is a miracle that one does not dissolve in one's bath like a lump of sugar."
>
> —pablo picasso (1881-1973), artist

from the heart

i believe in miracles. here are some that i've seen you do in the lives of others . . .

_____
_____
_____
_____
_____
_____

here are some of the miracles i see you doing in my life . . .

_____
_____
_____
_____
_____
_____

here are some of the miracles i long to see you do in the world . . .

_____
_____
_____
_____
_____
_____

What kind of miracles does God perform today? Does he still heal and cast out demons? What makes you think so? Read Hebrews 13:8 and reflect on God's power and ability to work in your life today.

"Now glory be to God! By his mighty power at work within us, he is able to accomplish infinitely more than we would ever dare to ask or hope. May he be given glory in the church and in Christ Jesus forever and ever through endless ages. Amen."

Ephesians 3:20, 21

ADORATION—a whole universe of praise echoes in that one word of worship. When I adore you, you bubble to the surface of who I am and all I know is your grace.

You're worthy of more praise than I could ever give, more glory than I could ever speak. Why is it so hard to break through the surface of the daily grind and see how alive and whole and real you are, beating like a second heart in the sea of air around me?

O God, I'm in awe of who you are but I don't know how to tell you! It's almost like language isn't big enough or broad enough or wide enough to hold in my thoughts of who you are. You're like a sea and my words are stones that drop into you and disappear. I don't feel like any of them ever really enter into your heart.

God, I'm humbled by thoughts of how great you are. You're so much greater than anything I could ever dream or imagine! Your power is beyond anything I could imagine. Your love is deeper than the oceans and wider than the sky. Your grace is willing to sacrifice all just to bring a smile to the face of your beloved. Your peace is beyond understanding. Your wisdom is beyond comprehension. You are endlessly great and glorious, surrounded by the purest light, filled with the most perfect love.

My soul bows in awe of you.

My heart trembles in fear.

My mind reels in wonder.

Lord, your greatness contrasts with my smallness and makes me feel insignificant, but to you I am precious. It's a mystery!

Your plans are glorious, your dreams are magnificent and your compassion is strong enough to break even the bonds of death.

I praise you and honor you and glorify your name. You alone, O God, deserve all honor, all praise, all glory, all majesty and all credit forever. Now, help me not just to say these things but to live them. Let the truths of who you are shape my attitudes, choices, thoughts and plans as I live my life in praise of you . . .

from the heart

I'm not very good at praising you. Right now, without words, I want to praise you for your mercy, love and compassion . . .

God, I'm in awe of your power. I'm speechless with wonder. Search my heart and see these joys you bring to me . . .

_____

_____

_____

Let all of my life resound with your praise. I haven't turned these areas of my life over to you yet, but here they are . . .

_____

_____

_____

deeper and further

Jesus' whole life was a song of praise to his Father. Read John 17:1-5. What did Jesus live for (see verses 2, 3)? To whom did Jesus live in obedience (verse 4)? What does that tell you about Jesus' attitude? How does that challenge your attitude?

"I have seen you in your sanctuary and gazed upon your power and glory. Your unfailing love is better to me than life itself; how I praise you! I will honor you as long as I live, lifting up my hands to you in prayer."

Psalm 63:2-4

THEY say your grace is amazing and I guess I'm finally beginning to understand what that means. When I earn something, it's not at all amazing when I get it . . . but when I deserve nothing and receive everything, then it truly is amazing after all.

The more I look at my life, the more amazing your grace appears. The more I see how often I hurt you by my thoughtless words, jealous spirit, selfish motives, argumentative replies, impatience, prejudice, pettiness, sensitivity, disobedience, rebellious nature, foul language, grudges, prying questions, resentment, unforgiveness and greed . . . the more I see this ocean of filth in my soul the more amazed I am by your grace and forgiveness that reaches down and washes me clean and says, "There now, that's how you were intended to be all along. Pure and perfect in my arms."

You forgive me! You offer me life, freedom and peace even though I've rebelled against you. Your grace is like a gentle calming fragrance that takes over and covers the stench of my sin so that all is refreshed within my soul and my spirit can breathe once again.

Grace.

I never really thought of grace as so amazing before . . .

"Your worst days are never so bad that you are beyond the reach of God's grace. And your best days are never so good that you are beyond the need of God's grace."
—jerry bridges, christian author, THE DISCIPLINE OF GRACE

from the heart

here's why i don't deserve your grace . . .

_____

_____

_____

here's what your grace means to me . . .

_____

_____

_____

here's how my life has been changed by your grace . . .

_____

_____

_____

here's how i want to thank you for your grace . . .

_____

_____

_____

deeper and further

Read Luke 7:36-50. What does Jesus say the secret to great love is? How come it's so hard to get to the place of great love? Where does grace fit into this story? Who do you identify with in this story, the woman who had great love, or the religious leader who had little love? What needs to change in your heart before you can love Jesus more?

"For it is by grace you have been saved, through faith—and this not from yourselves, it is the gift of God—not by works, so that no one can boast."

Ephesians 2:8, 9 NIV

I WANT to give you something lasting for all you've given me. I want to offer you a gift, but everything I try to bring you already came from you. As I look within myself, I find that you are the source of all that's good in my life. All I have to offer you, you've already given. So my giving is nothing but an act of returning to you the gifts you so freely offer.

Breath is a gift. Life is a gift. Health is a gift. Even my dreams and my desires, my hopes and my plans, my worship and my praise; they're all gifts from you. Even the desire to please you comes from you. And yet, you accept all my offerings!

Though they are tainted.

Spoiled.

Cracked and splintered.

To you they are a pleasure! To you they are a treasure!

I'm more in awe of you than ever. And I say, take me as I am! All of me! I guess the way to thank you for all you've done for me—I mean **really** *thank you—is to start living less for myself and more for you. Let me live for you!*

Show me what needs to change in my life. Help me to live out my faith in you. Let that be my way of saying thanks for all you've done for me. Look at my motives and see my desire to honor you, look at my choices and see my commitment to obeying you.

Change me so that I become more of what you require, and less of what I desire.

And when I fail, when I fall down or stumble, lift me back up. Set me on the path of righteousness again. Take my hand and lead me . . .

"In gratitude for your own good fortune you must render in return some sacrifice of your life for other life."

—albert schweitzer (1875-1965), humanitarian, medical missionary for nearly 50 years

from the heart

i will no longer hold back these parts of my life from you . . .

_____
_____
_____

here are three things i don't typically thank you for, but i'd like to thank you for today . . .

1. _____
2. _____
3. _____

God, here's how i'd like to show my thanks for all you've done for me . . .

_____
_____
_____

deeper and further

Read Psalm 40:6-8. What does God delight in—religious sacrifices or heartfelt obedience? Why is it so much easier to bring him religious service than obedience? How will knowing what God desires affect your life? How does it affect the way you'll thank God for all he has done?

"And now, just as you accepted Christ Jesus as your Lord, you must continue to live in obedience to him. Let your roots grow down into him and draw up nourishment from him, so you will grow in faith, strong and vigorous in the truth you were taught. Let your lives overflow with thanksgiving for all he has done."

Colossians 2:6, 7

I AM in awe of you.

I think I know all about love, but most of my love is tainted by my own selfishness. I love so that others might love me back . . . I give just to feel good about myself or balance the scales . . . I flatter so that I can control and manipulate other people. Sometimes I wonder if I even love anything at all. At least, anything other than myself!

*But the purity of **your** love amazes me! You give without manipulating, you offer all of yourself with no strings attached, you serve for the sake of service itself and not for any ulterior motives. Your love is unfailing! And that love has sought me!*

Father, you loved so you gave.

Spirit, you loved so you came.

Jesus, you loved so you died.

What kind of love is this? A love so pure and perfect that it cannot help but die for its beloved. A love so everlasting that eternity is swallowed up in its wings . . . a love so unfailing that it remains faithful through a thousand betrayals . . . a love so tender that it washes away the tears of the world . . . a love so powerful that it breaks the teeth of death and conquers all the powers of darkness . . .

Teach me to love like you love! A love like yours is beyond anything I could ever understand. It's a love I can't grasp or define or even vaguely imagine. But it's a love I can receive! And it's a love I can know, and because of it, I can worship you.

And so I do.

To think that the same mind that dreamed up the galaxies and spoke them into existence actually dreamed of me humbles me beyond words. To think that my name is on your lips and my face is in your heart and my dreams are on your mind . . . how can this be?

O God, your love humbles and astounds me!

The human language doesn't contain words or ways that can begin to thank you for your crystal clear, conquering, perfect, unchangeable, sacrificial love.

But know my heart, O God. Find your thanks there.

from the heart

God, here's what i'd compare your love to . . .

_____

_____

_____

Spirit, here's how i'd like to show you my thanks . . .

_____

_____

_____

Jesus, this is how i'd describe your love to someone who doesn't know you . . .

_____

_____

_____

deeper and further

Look up 1 John 4:7, 8, 16. More than any characteristic, what is God? According to these verses, how does that naturally affect his followers? How does it affect you? How does this view of life change your perspective on other people?

"See how very much our heavenly Father loves us, for he allows us to be called his children, and we really are! But the people who belong to this world don't know God, so they don't understand that we are his children."

1 John 3:1

I DON'T know what to believe about prayer. Sometimes I don't know what to pray for and sometimes, to be honest, it doesn't seem to me like you care about my prayers or that you're even listening.

*But now, this time, I see that you **are** listening! Because the thing I prayed for actually came true! Part of me wants to chalk it up to circumstances or coincidences or something like that. But I know, in a deep and secret place in my soul, that you really did answer my prayer.*

And that thought blows my mind!

You care about me that much!

You're amazing, God, and I thank you for who you are and all you've done for me!

God, it's all about you. You're the author of my faith, writing it upon my heart—and the finisher of my faith, bringing it to completion through Jesus.

You're the one I live for, you're the one I desire above all others. You're the first to me and the last, the A-Z, the entire reason for being and breathing and living.

Or at least, that's what I want. That's what I want to be true. That's how I want to live. And when I feel drained of you and tired of the journey, and sorry for my past failures and mistakes, overwhelm me again with yourself.

And reveal to me that it's all about you, once again. Answer this prayer for me and let it define all of my life . . .

> "As is the business of tailors to make clothes and cobblers to make shoes, so it is the business of Christians to pray."
> —martin luther (1483-1546), German educator, translator, reformer of the church

from the heart

this is what i prayed for . . .

_____

_____

_____

here's how you answered my prayer . . .

_____

_____

_____

here's another prayer request i've been wanting to bring to you . . .

_____

_____

_____

deeper and further

What promises do we have concerning prayer? What does God require of us when we approach him in prayer? Check out Mark 11:22-25 and Philippians 4:6, 7 for some answers and insights into the principles of prayer and the role of prayer in the life of a believer.

"But if you stay joined to me and my words remain in you, you may ask any request you like, and it will be granted!"

John 15:7

"AND this is the way to have eternal life—to know you, the only true God, and Jesus Christ, the one you sent to earth."

John 17:3

from the gut

God, once again you've taken care of me! Once again you've helped me when I didn't deserve it! Now I'm here to say thanks and also to ask you for the humility to rest more fully in your arms. I need lots of help doing that—letting myself become complete by letting myself be filled with you.

I don't like the idea of being taken care of. I like taking care of things myself—and getting the credit for them myself. But when it comes to salvation and my relationship with you, there's nothing I can do on my own. It's all you, God. You get the credit and I'll be honest, I wish I could take at least a little bit of the credit, but I can't. That's not easy to admit because pride is more alive in me than I usually let on.

God, I'm just starting to discover—really discover—what it means to know you. It's not really what I thought at the beginning.

Two things are happening at once in my heart. First, I'm seeing more clearly how much I need you. And second, I'm learning how deeply I've hurt you. The closer I come to you, the farther I realize I've wandered, the more pain I see I've caused, the deeper I see I've fallen and the greater I see I've sinned. It hurts to see all that, but it also refreshes me. Because I know once again that you have taken care of me, rescued me and saved me.

Spirit, the more I fall in love with you, the more I realize you fell in love with me first . . .

> "You may never know that Jesus is all you need, until Jesus is all you have."
> —corrie ten boom (1892-1983), nazi concentration camp survivor

from the heart

here's how you helped me . . .

_____

_____

_____

here's what you're doing right now in my life . . .

_____

_____

_____

here are the places i see evidence of your love . . .

_____

_____

_____

deeper and further

Check out Ephesians 3:20. How much is God able to do through you? Are you willing to let him? Are you willing to let him totally direct your life? What changes do you need to make in your habits and lifestyle to let him do that?

"I prayed to the LORD, and he answered me, freeing me from all my fears."

Psalm 34:4

JESUS knew there'd be times in our lives when we would step off the path and go where we're not supposed to go. He knew we'd be lured by the forbidden and enticed by the very signs that say "Keep Out," even if it's only our thoughts that go astray. And yet . . .

He has not punished us for all our sins, nor does he deal with us as we deserve. For his unfailing love toward those who fear him is as great as the height of the heavens above the earth. He has removed our rebellious acts as far away from us as the east is from the west. (Psalm 103:10-12)

When God forgives you . . . when he looks down from Heaven and purifies you . . . when he removes your unrighteousness from you . . . when he carries your guilt away . . . how can you help but respond with thanksgiving and humility? How can you help but be blown away when you consider instead the extent of his grace? We've deserved God's anger, but he has extended his love to us and "removed our rebellious acts."

Did you know that even though God knows everything, he's also very forgetful? How can that be? Well, look at what he says in Hebrews 8:12:

And I will forgive their wrongdoings, and I will never again remember their sins.

God forgives and he forgets. How does that make you feel? How is that gonna change your life?

from the gut

Lord, I'm human. With all the dignity that comes from being made in your image, with all the hope that comes from being redeemed, but with all of the scars on my heart that come from being a rebel.

God, I need two things from you. I need you to (1) show me clearly how much I've messed up, and (2) show me how perfectly you forgive me!

How should I respond when I realize that you've truly and totally forgiven me? What should I say? What do I do?

Thanks!

Is it really true? Do you really forgive and forget? I like to think I forgive people, but I don't forget. I remember. I'm an expert at that. I like to hold onto the past so I can bring it back up when I need to pull out the heavy artillery. But you don't. You forgive and you forget.

You forget?!

How can you forget? How can you wipe something that terrible and ugly and hurtful from your memory? But you do! You do!

You forget the words I spoke without thinking. You forget the deeds I did in the dark. You forget the dirty thoughts that mar and wither my soul.

You forget!

O God, I don't know exactly how to respond or what to say. I'm humbled by the knowledge that I deserve your anger, but receive your love . . . I deserve your guilt, but I get your grace . . . I deserve separation from you, but am invited instead into your presence . . .

Your gifts and your grace, your love and your forgiveness give me more peace than I've ever known. And all I want to do is praise you with all of who I am!

"I would rather live on the verge of falling and let my security be in the all sufficiency of the grace of God than to live in some kind of pietistic illusion of moral excellence. Not that I don't want to be morally excellent. But my faith isn't in the idea that I'm more moral than anyone else, my faith is in the idea that God and his love are greater than any sins that any of us commit."

–rich mullins (1955-1997), christian singer and songwriter

from the heart

here's where i've crossed the line . . .

_____
_____
_____
_____
_____
_____

here's how i feel about your forgiveness . . .

_____
_____
_____
_____
_____
_____

here's what i would compare your forgiveness to . . .

_____
_____
_____
_____
_____
_____

deeper and further

Read Psalm 32:3-7. Can you follow the progression of David's feelings with himself and with God? What brings about the huge change in his life (see verse 5)? If God did that with David, can he do it for you, too?

"Oh, what joy for those whose rebellion is forgiven, whose sin is put out of sight!"

Psalm 32:1

prayers
of
truth

SAMSON was always out for revenge.

God had called him to be a great deliverer for his people. God put him in the right place at the right time, gave him opportunities to fight his foes, empowered him with superhuman strength and filled him with the Holy Spirit. Samson performed amazing feats of strength and was a fierce and mighty warrior.

But all along the way, Samson kept getting sidetracked by his own personal feelings of how he had been wronged. While God wanted him to deliver the nation, Samson took everything personally. When the Philistines (Samson's archenemies) murdered his wife, he vowed he would get revenge. Here's how he put it:

"Because you did this," Samson vowed, "I will take my revenge on you, and I won't stop until I'm satisfied!" (Judges 15:7)

As a result, even though he was used by God in mighty ways, he never locked into doing things God's way. Not totally. Not fully. And he never reached his full potential as a warrior and a leader. Vengeance drained his energies and distorted his perspective.

Feeling wronged and slighted or angry and vengeful is pretty common for most of us. When we're wronged, we hold onto this idea of getting revenge, like Samson did. We want to get even. But God has another method in mind. Here's God's advice to follow instead of taking revenge:

1. Take it to God in prayer. *(see Matthew 5:44)*
2. Hold your anger in check. *(see Romans 12:17)*
3. Seek peace wherever possible. *(see Romans 12:18)*
4. Leave the situation in God's hands. *(see Romans 12:19)*
5. Respond with compassion. *(see Proverbs 25:21)*
6. Overcome evil with good. *(see Romans 12:21)*

Where are you in this process? What steps have you taken? Which steps do you need to put into practice?

God, there haven't been many times in my life when I've been so mad. Or when I've wanted so badly to get even with someone. But now! When you've been hurt like I've been hurt all you can think of is getting revenge!

They say vengeance is the Lord's and that we're supposed to let you repay wrongs. But God, why is that? It almost doesn't seem fair. You get to take all the revenge? What are we supposed to do, just sit here and be doormats?

I'm sorry. I don't mean to question you. It's just that I'm so upset and it's hard to see clearly through all this anger.

Jesus, you said to pray for those who persecute us . . . I don't know if I can do this. It's gonna be hard to stay angry at someone you're praying for, but here I go . . . God please bless _____. Show 'em forgiveness.

Take the desire for vengeance from my heart. Melt the anger and hatred away. And let me respond with the same attitude of Jesus, not Samson . . .

> "I say, love your enemies! Pray for those who persecute you!"
> —Jesus of nazareth (matthew 5:44)

"The Master said, 'If out of the three hundred SONGS I had to take one phrase to cover all my teaching, I would say, 'Let there be no evil in your thoughts.'"
—THE ANALECTS OF CONFUCIUS, book ii, 3 (written about 500 B.C.)

from the heart

here's how i was hurt . . .

_____

_____

_____

_____

_____

_____

here's why i wanna take revenge . . .

_____

_____

_____

_____

_____

_____

here's how i need you to help me right now . . .

_____

_____

_____

_____

_____

_____

What lies at the core of our desire for revenge? Is it a desire for what's best for ourselves, or the other person? If God doesn't want us to take revenge, then where do all these vengeful thoughts come from? Could they even possibly be from him? Why or why not? Read Romans 12:17-21. How do these verses change your perspective on getting revenge?

"Dear friends, never avenge yourselves. Leave that to God. For it is written, 'I will take vengeance; I will repay those who deserve it' says the Lord."

Romans 12:19

GOD, I'm sick of it. I just don't see any point to being good any longer. Other people have all kinds of fun doing whatever they want (basically all the stuff I'm not supposed to do). And all the while I just tell myself not to act that way, because you've told me not to. So I sit out. And the deal is, I sometimes start thinking, "If you forgive me anyway, why shouldn't I just go ahead and do that stuff? I mean, what harm would there be in having a little fun sometimes?"

Right now, I just don't see any advantage to being good. Sometimes I get bored with it—with church and being good—the whole deal.

God, I know you want me to act certain ways. I know all that. And I know what's right and what's wrong. At least most of the time I do. The tough part isn't in knowing, it's in doing. 'Cause there are plenty of times when I feel like doing the stuff I know is wrong.

And right now is one of 'em.

I don't see any advantage to being good. All I see are the attractions to the pleasures of sin.

So, anyway, that's why I'm talking to you. 'Cause I know you care and I know you're the only one who can help. Change this around for me, okay? Help me to see that my life needs to grow out of a rich relationship with you. Help me understand that obedience isn't for me, it's for you. And obedience isn't a way to earn Heaven, it's a way of saying thanks for the gift of faith.

Show me that obedience isn't a way of paying you back, but a natural response for having all of my debt already paid off. Start there and get me going on the right track again . . .

> "The world is not ruined by the wickedness of the wicked, but by the weakness of the good."
>
> —napoleon bonaparte (1769-1821), french emperor and statesman

from the heart

these are the lies about "being good" that i believe most often . . .

_____

_____

_____

this is the main reason i sometimes feel like bailing on you . . .

_____

_____

_____

Jesus, here's something i've been meaning to tell you but haven't gotten around to saying . . .

_____

_____

_____

deeper and further

Read John 15:9-11. What should motivate us toward obedience? If you don't feel like obeying Jesus, what's lacking in your life? (Hint, see 1 John 5:2!)

"This is love for God: to obey his commands. And his commands are not burdensome, for everyone born of God overcomes the world. This is the victory that has overcome the world, even our faith. Who is it that overcomes the world? Only he who believes that Jesus is the Son of God."

1 John 5:3-5 NIV

~132

WE all know we're not supposed to do wrong things, but Jesus even warned against thinking wrong things. He also cautioned against doing the right thing for the wrong reasons. For example, in Jesus' day some people would look for a good public place to pray. They'd pray aloud so other people could hear how holy they were. Well, Jesus said that when you pray you shouldn't look for an audience at all, but instead shut yourself up in a private place with God:

But when you pray, go away by yourself, shut the door behind you, and pray to your Father secretly. Then your Father, who knows all secrets, will reward you. (Matthew 6:6)

It's like Jesus is saying, "Being godly isn't a show. It's about having an intimate conversation with God." When you pray, honestly ask yourself these questions: "Who is my audience? Whose approval do I seek? What rewards do I desire?"

In Jesus' day, some people would go without food (a practice called "fasting") as a means of relying more on God (not as a way of losing weight!). He told those who chose to fast to make sure they didn't look sickly or tired or anything so no one would suspect that they were going without food. It was supposed to be just between them and God.

Jesus mentioned the same kind of stuff in regard to giving money at the offering plate. You see, God isn't interested at all in an outward show of holiness if there isn't an inner reliance on him. Don't even bother if you're just going through the motions of going to church or being nice, acting "religious" just to look good, to keep up appearances or impress people. It might fool your friends, but it's not gonna fool God.

If prayer or Bible study is just a habit that you have or a ritual you've picked up somewhere along the line, don't even bother doing it—that kind of activity makes God sick.

God looks deep into the heart.

It takes a lot of guts to admit that you haven't always had the right reasons for the right actions. But when you get to that place of honesty, God never looks away. Instead he welcomes you, accepts you and surrounds you with his presence, forgiveness and guidance.

> "It is not difficult to avoid death, gentlemen of the jury, it is much more difficult to avoid wickedness, for it runs faster than death."
>
> —socrates (469-399 B.C.) in APOLOGY

from the gut

God, sometimes I feel like an actor playing a part. It's almost like I step into my role every day and the play begins.

I act one way, but feel another. I say one thing, but think another. I'm like a lake where everyone sees the surface, but beneath the surface there are currents going in all kinds of deadly directions.

I'm not pure. Not really. The times I think I'm pure I usually have an ulterior motive. There's no honesty in me. Not really. It's just an act so that I can get what I want. And all of the nice stuff I do is usually done to help someone look good—me. It's all for me!

I have these goals: I want people to like me. I want people to admire me. I want to get people to act in a certain way. I like feeling good and sometimes I don't care who I hurt when I do it.

I'm sorry, God!

I sometimes think I'm ready to die for you, but am I even ready to live for you? I guess that's the bigger question, isn't it? Who am I living for, myself or you? You said we must deny ourselves and follow you, but so often I catch myself doing the opposite—disobeying you and going my own way instead. Help me to walk in step with the Spirit. Help me to live that out. Step by step, stride by stride. Not trying to get the Spirit to walk in step with me!

Purify my life from the inside out. I know it has to start in the heart. So start there.

Fill my heart with yourself, O God! For where you are, nothing evil can dwell. Nothing vile can grow. Nothing impure can exist. So take over the garden of my heart, uproot the selfishness, weed out the greed, till the soil and plant fresh seeds of faith.

Help me to start forgetting myself and start living with real love, from the heart! And help me start today . . .

> "The one and only spiritual disease is thinking one is well."
> —g. k. chesterton (1874-1936), poet, novelist and critic

from the heart

Jesus, here are some areas of my life where i haven't been real with you . . .

_____

_____

_____

_____

Spirit, convict me when i start to do this stuff for the wrong reasons . . .

_____

_____

_____

_____

Father, forgive me for . . .

_____

_____

_____

_____

Read Proverbs 20:27. How many of our hidden motives does God uncover? How does that make you feel? Why do you think we try so hard to hide our motives and excuse ourselves? What impure priorities do you need to bring to God right now? How can you practically give those to him and walk in his Spirit? (see Galatians 5:25)

"But you desire honesty from the heart, so you can teach me to be wise in my inmost being."

Psalm 51:6

NAOMI couldn't let go of her past. When her husband and two sons died, she became resentful with God. When she returned to her hometown, everyone was surprised to see her. "Look!" they cried, "it's Naomi!" But look at Naomi's response (the word "Mara" means "bitter"):

"Don't call me Naomi," she told them. "Instead, call me Mara, for the Almighty has made life very bitter for me. I went away full, but the LORD has brought me home empty. Why should you call me Naomi when the LORD has caused me to suffer and the Almighty has sent such tragedy?" (Ruth 1:20, 21)

Yikes. This woman had issues.

Well, as the story progresses, Naomi's daughter-in-law (a young lady named Ruth) gets married to a kind man named Boaz and they have a baby. When the baby is born, though, the women of the town bring the child to Naomi so she can help raise him, because they saw God's work behind the scenes in providing this son. And they don't call her Mara anymore.

Naomi took care of the baby and cared for him as if he were her own. The neighbor women said, "Now at last Naomi has a son again!" (Ruth 4:16, 17)

Sometimes life throws us a curve. Sometimes tragedy strikes. Sometimes regrets won't leave us alone. Sometimes we make choices that don't seem to let us move on. Either way, if the past seems to slither into your life and wrap itself around you, remember the story of Naomi. God was still in charge of the present even though Naomi found it hard to move on from the past.

And just like God blessed Naomi and gave her a fresh start, God can set you free from past bitterness, shame and guilt, too.

Here's the thing. I've done stuff and I've said stuff that I just can't seem to forget. My guilt lurks there on the sidelines of my memory, laughing at me, taunting me.

God, it's like my past reaches toward me with these tentacles that control me. And entangle me. And strangle me. These slimy regrets surface again and again, reminding me—always reminding me—of my choices. My failures. My mistakes—all right, I'll say it, my sins.

I know some of my choices have consequences that still affect me and that's the way it is in this world. But I need your help to be free from my resentments and regrets and from the pain of the past that crawls up into today and won't go away.

Free me, O Savior! Forgive me! Rule in my heart! Cut the cords of the past and show me the freedom that comes from forgiveness. Let me live in the grace of each moment, neither chained to the past nor afraid of the future.

Let me see to the horizon again! Let me drink in beauty again! Let me watch with delicate wonder as life circles around me! It's only forgiveness and guidance that will free me. It's only your love that can let me live again. That much I know. Do your work in my heart . . .

"Forget past mistakes. Forget failures. Forget everything except what you're going to do now, and do it."

—william durant (1861-1947), founder of general motors corporation

from the heart

here are some of the choices that still haunt me . . .

_____
_____
_____
_____
_____
_____

here are some of the ways i need you to cut my entanglements
with the past . . .

_____
_____
_____
_____
_____
_____

here's a past hurt that i'm ready to hand over to you once and for
all . . .

_____
_____
_____
_____
_____
_____

Moses probably thought he'd never return to Egypt again. He'd spent the last 40 years working as a shepherd. By the time God spoke to Moses at the burning bush, he was already a senior citizen. He was probably ready to retire, but God had a different plan. Read about it in Exodus 3, 4.

When God looks at our lives, he's more concerned with whether we're serving, honoring and following him *now* than if we used to in the past. Don't let the past control you. God's desire is to use you, bless you and to direct your paths today.

"No, dear brothers and sisters, I am still not all I should be, but I am focusing all my energies on this one thing: Forgetting the past and looking forward to what lies ahead, I strain to reach the end of the race and receive the prize for which God, through Christ Jesus, is calling us up to heaven."

Philippians 3:13, 14

GOD, I'm so quick to feel insulted, passed over, put down. I'm so quick to demand that life treats me fairly. I'm so quick to defend myself and look down on others and judge 'em, but then get offended when they judge me! I'm so convinced that I'm always right and that I deserve what's best and that life should always lean in my direction. I'm easily offended and angered. I'm impatient when things don't go my way, and quick to complain about my problems. I desire what I shouldn't have, but I envy people for what they have . . .

And yet, it's so, so hard for me to say "I'm sorry" and to admit "I was wrong!"

God, what's wrong with me?

I'm so tempted to think of myself as a pretty good person, as better than most people, as not so bad after all. It all sounds so true when I say those words to myself; it seems so real. But God! Help me to know that it's my excuses that led Christ to die, my pride that nailed him to the cross, my sins that left him there to suffer, my rebellion that caused him to cry out in agony.

God, it was my fault! And all those fine-sounding excuses are subtle lies that lead me farther from the truth, farther from you.

God, here's the truth of the matter—I'd rather cover up my wrongs than admit them. I'd rather hide from my past than face it. I'd rather ignore my mistakes than learn from them. I guess it's because I don't like the prospect of humbling myself enough to admit my wrongs and then move on to receiving forgiveness. I'm afraid of the consequences. I hate that feeling of not being right. It all boils down to pride.

Change me, God!

Give me the newness of your Spirit and the honesty of the soul to admit, repent, change and grow. Expose my sin, God! Whatever it takes, draw me closer to you. Destroy my pride!

Whatever you need to rip out of my life or replace in my life or weave into my life, do it. I'm ready to go deeper. I'm ready to accept

*whatever comes from your hand because I know that whatever you
send is a gift that'll lead me closer to the truth. Even if it hurts. Even if
it exposes me for what I really am.*

*I pray for the humility to honor you, the will to serve you and the
grace to please you right now . . .*

> "We can easily forgive a child who is afraid of the dark, but one of the great
> tragedies of life is men who are afraid of the light."
>
> —plato (428-347 B.C.), greek philosopher

from the heart

here are some of the things i've done that i need to tell you about . . .

_____

_____

_____

_____

_____

here's why i hate admitting when i'm wrong . . .

_____

_____

_____

_____

_____

here's what needs to happen for you to teach me humility . . .

_____

_____

_____

_____

_____

It never feels good to admit we've done something wrong. What are the issues that get in the way of admitting our wrongs? What emotions or attitudes play a factor? Read Mark 7:21-23. In verse 23 what does Jesus say about pride (or arrogance)? How are you going to respond to this truth?

"People who cover over their sins will not prosper. But if they confess and forsake them, they will receive mercy."

Proverbs 28:13

IT didn't seem like a big deal at the time. I just told myself that it wasn't really that bad and that my teacher is always unfair anyway and that everyone else cheats, too. But all those excuses don't seem to help anymore.

God, there's so much pressure to get good grades and do well in school! And my life is so busy and full and I never seem to have enough time to get all my homework done. Cheating seems like such an easy answer. And it doesn't seem all that bad compared to big stuff like murder . . . and people almost never get caught, so . . .

What I'm trying to say is, it's an easy trap to get sucked into.

But God, you despise cheating! You would never cheat! You would never condone cheating! I knew that and still I did it!

God, I'm so sorry. I really am!

You hate all forms of lying and dishonesty, God. Extinguish my excuses and show me how deeply cheating offends you. Then, forgive me. Wipe my wrongs away. And give me the guts to do what's right, to choose what's right and to pursue what's right. If that means admitting to my teacher what I've done, help me do it. No matter what, I know I need to serve you. Show me what that means in the big things and little things in life. And then, give me the guts to live it out. Every day . . .

> "Uncorrected errors will multiply. Someone once asked me if there wasn't benefit in overlooking one small flaw. 'What is a small flaw?' I asked him."
> —don shula, legendary NFL football coach

from the heart

here's how i cheated . . .

_____

_____

_____

here's why i cheated in the first place . . .

_____

_____

_____

here's what i need to do now . . .

_____

_____

_____

deeper and further

In ancient times, a common way of cheating was to have scales that were weighted so that you could make more money off your customers. What does Proverbs 11:1 say about honesty and balanced scales? What application does that verse have for today?

"Since you have heard all about him and have learned the truth that is in Jesus, throw off your old evil nature and your former way of life, which is rotten through and through, full of lust and deception. Instead, there must be a spiritual renewal of your thoughts and attitudes. You must display a new nature because you are a new person, created in God's likeness—righteous, holy, and true. So put away all falsehood and 'tell your neighbor the truth' because we belong to each other."

Ephesians 4:21-25

IT'S easy to lie. Almost second nature for me sometimes.

I lie when I'm hurting and I don't want anyone else to know about it. When people ask me how I'm doing, I say, "good," even when I'm not, even when I feel hurt or sad or hopeful or angry, I just tell 'em, "I'm fine."

I lie when I'm worried people will think less of me for who I really am. "Didn't you think that was an awesome movie?" they say and I mumble, "Yeah, I guess so." When I really thought it was stupid.

I lie when I'm afraid of the consequences of telling the truth. "Were you looking at her paper?!" the teacher asks. "No way!" I say. When I was.

Sometimes I lie to get ahead or to impress people or to look good. Or I lie to hide who I really am or how I really feel or what I was really doing. Sometimes I lie to make other people feel good, by complimenting them when I feel like laughing at them.

I even lie to myself sometimes when I make excuses for the things I do when I tell myself it wasn't really so bad.

Any way you cut it, I lie a lot. I probably lie as much as I tell the truth. Sometimes more.

And I've done it again.

It scares me because Jesus always told the truth and he called Satan "the father of lies." I don't want that kind of a father. I don't want anything to do with his family.

Forgive me, God. For all the lies. Give me the desire to tell the truth and the guts to do it. Even when it hurts . . .

"I am the way and the truth and the life. . . . Everyone on the side of truth listens to me."

—Jesus of nazareth (john 14:6; 18:37 NIV)

> "Mother always told me, if you tell a lie, always rehearse it. It if don't sound good to you, it won't sound good to no one else."
> —satchel paige (1906-1982), hall of fame major league pitcher

from the heart

God, i'm most tempted to lie when . . .

_____

_____

_____

_____

_____

i'll work hard at telling the truth by . . .

_____

_____

_____

_____

_____

deeper and further

Jesus said he was "the Truth" (John 14:6) and he said that "the truth will set you free" (John 8:32). What does that tell you about lies? If you put these two sayings together, who do you discover will set you free? Who (or what) puts you into bondage? How does that make you feel about Jesus?

"You spread out our sins before you—our secret sins—and you see them all."

Psalm 90:8

FOR a long time, David thought he'd gotten away with it. He figured that since he was the king, he was untouchable. He had an affair with a married woman and it looked like no one was the wiser.

But then, she found out she was pregnant.

So first, David tried to ignore the problem. Then he tried to cover it all up. But when those things didn't work, he took steps to bury the problem forever by getting rid of the lady's husband (by arranging for him to be killed). Finally, he pretended that nothing bad had happened at all and married the widow, Bathsheba.

But none of that worked. God knew all about David's wrongdoings and he sent the prophet Nathan to confront him. Finally, David had to come clean.

"I have sinned against the Lord," he said. And Nathan assured David of God's forgiveness. As David looked back on the moment, he wrote,

Purify me from my sins, and I will be clean; wash me, and I will be whiter than snow. Oh, give me back my joy again; you have broken me—now let me rejoice. Don't keep looking at my sins. Remove the stain of my guilt. (Psalm 51:7-9)

No matter what you've done, God can forgive you. No matter how far you've strayed, God can bring you home again. No matter how stained your soul, he can make it pure and white again.

"Come now, let us argue this out," says the LORD. "No matter how deep the stain of your sins, I can remove it. I can make you as clean as freshly fallen snow. Even if you are stained as red as crimson, I can make you as white as wool." (Isaiah 1:18)

The forgiveness God gave to David is the same he offers to you— full and free and forever.

purify me

How can you love me? How can you forgive me when I should know better, should do better, should be better?

When I look at my life, all I see are the depths of my selfishness and the truth about how terrible I've been. O God! You know this thing that I've done. You know how unspeakable it is. And you know how much guilt I'm carrying.

Forgive me, Father.

Cleanse me, Spirit.

Accept me, Jesus.

God, you're a consuming fire. There's nothing neutral about a consuming fire. It does what it wants and it moves where it likes and you better get out of the way unless you wanna be consumed. But right now I need you to consume me! I don't wanna run away and hide! Sweep over me and ignite me! Burn my sin away!

Consume me, O God! Purify me! Burn away all that is unacceptable until only my love for you and my life in you remain . . .

no more hiding

God, it's me.

Again.

I know that the last time I did this I told you it'd be the last time. I know I promised you I'd never do it again. And still, after all that, I've messed up.

I tried my hardest but it didn't help! And now I'm back in that place somewhere between guilt and forgiveness where I just yearn for your peace.

Everybody these days is telling me to feel good about myself. Like that's the solution for all my problems. But how should I feel when I've done something I know I shouldn't feel good about? What then?

I mean, I've done stuff that makes me feel rotten deep down inside and just "trying to feel good about myself" seems like such a shallow answer. Is that the best advice the world has to offer?

I know that's not the answer!

I've looked deeply into my heart and I don't like what I see. My heart is dark and ugly and the sin runs deep. And I can't deny it any longer. And I guess, even if I can't admit it to anyone else, I can tell you. I finally see how horrible I can be. How wrong I've been.

I can't stand what I see! Are other people's souls as stained as mine? Are other people's selfish desires as strong as mine? Are other people's goals as greedy as mine?

Forgive me, Lord. My heart has been in love with the darkness. But now, I seek you and the light of your truth . . .

"Every sin is more hurtful to the sinner than to the sinned against."
—saint augustine (354-430) from ENCHIRIDION ON FAITH, HOPE, AND LOVE

from the heart

here's what i need you to forgive:

_____
_____
_____
_____
_____

here's how i feel about what i did . . .

_____
_____
_____
_____
_____

in my own words, here's how i feel about your assurance of forgiveness . . .

_____

_____

_____

_____

_____

deeper and further

Read 1 John 1:8-10. How many of your wrongs does this verse say God is willing to forgive? What does that mean for you right now? How pure does complete forgiveness make you in the sight of God—ten percent, 50 percent, 100 percent? How does that make you feel?

"Wash me clean from my guilt. Purify me from my sin. For I recognize my shameful deeds—they haunt me day and night."
Psalm 51:2, 3

TELLING people about Jesus can be intimidating. What if they ask you a question you can't answer? Or bring up an objection you hadn't thought about? What if they insult you because of your lack of knowledge?

That happened to a man whom Jesus healed of blindness. The religious leaders peppered him with questions and accusations. He didn't debate with them. He didn't preach to them. He even refused to argue with them. All he did was tell them what Jesus had done for him. When the leaders called Jesus a sinner, he responded,

"I don't know whether he is a sinner," the man replied. "But I know this: I was blind, and now I can see!" (John 9:25)

The evidence this man presented was his changed life, not fancy theological arguments. And that drove the religious scholars crazy!

Think about it. When you introduce your friends to each other you don't hand out resumes and say, "I'd like you to consider having a friendship with this person. Here are her qualifications . . ." Instead, you share what that person means to you, what she has done for you, how she has helped or listened or supported or stuck with you.

Those are the things that matter.

People might argue about this or that theological point, but nobody can argue with a changed life!

The teachings of the church are like God's resume. They're necessary for clearly understanding who God is, what he's like and what he's done. But the best place to start in sharing his love is by telling others what he has done for you personally. The resume can come later.

Your goal is never to argue someone into God's kingdom, it's to love 'em in. Just like Jesus did. Every person matters to God. He did all he could to rescue us, now he asks us to share his love and the message of his love with others.

Dear Jesus, I want to share your love with others. I really do, but I don't always know what to say. I'm scared sometimes of how I'll come across—like, will they think I'm some kind of religious fanatic or something? Will they stop liking me? What if I say something that offends them?

I get tangled up with all of these questions and excuses and it seems like I never get around to actually sharing my faith at all. Sometimes, the things I've said or done in the past haunt me.

Give me boldness and confidence and humility to tell others about you!

Give me a deep and burning passion to share your truths with gentleness, compassion and love.

And no matter how people respond, let me be satisfied in this alone: that I was faithful to you.

from the heart

here's someone i've been afraid to share my faith with:

_____

these are the things i'm afraid will happen if i try to share my faith . . .

_____

_____

_____

here's how i think you want me to share my faith . . .

_____

_____

_____

The message of God's love is offensive. Why? Because humans are so blinded by pride that we want to feel like we've earned Heaven on our own, by our own hard work or good deeds. Read Titus 3:4-7.

Who gets the credit for the salvation of believers? Can we take any credit for our faith at all? Why do you say that? How does that affect your view of yourself, God and witnessing? How does 1 Peter 3:15, 16 say we should tell others about Jesus?

"We are confident of all this because of our great trust in God through Christ. It is not that we think we can do anything of lasting value by ourselves. Our only power and success come from God. He is the one who has enabled us to represent his new covenant."

2 Corinthians 3:4-6

GOD, some things are like magnets to my heart. I know everyone struggles with different stuff—gossiping, greed, anger, pride, lust, envy, hatred, breaking their promises, unforgiveness. All that stuff. Well, I struggle, too!

And I know Jesus doesn't just want outward obedience without any internal obedience. You're just as disappointed in me for fantasizing about sex as going off and doing it. And holding a grudge is the same type of sin as murder, because both grow from the same seeds of hatred.

But God, I'm drawn toward some things that I know are wrong! And even though I know I'll regret it, I end up doing that stuff anyway!

God, give me self-control to say "no" to those things, and to say "yes" to you . . . "yes" all the way down in my heart. O Spirit, blow through the wasteland of my dreams! Sweep through the wreckage of the past! Give me your peace, and make me yours. Make all of me yours. All yours . . .

Increase my faith so that you can increase my desire, ability and power to obey you . . .

"And when you gaze long into an abyss, the abyss gazes also into you."
—friedrich nietzsche (1844-1900), an atheist german philosopher who eventually went insane

from the heart

here's the temptation i struggle with the most . . .

_____

_____

_____

here's what i'll do the next time i'm tempted . . .

_____

_____

_____

here's my plan for avoiding tempting situations in the first place . . .

_____

_____

_____

deeper and further

Hebrews 4:14-16 explains why Jesus is qualified to help us through any temptation. What reason (or reasons) are given in these verses? How does that make you feel about bringing your problems to Jesus?

"For the grace of God has been revealed, bringing salvation to all people. And we are instructed to turn from godless living and sinful pleasures. We should live in this evil world with self-control, right conduct, and devotion to God."

Titus 2:11, 12

I KNEW we were getting into dangerous territory. I knew we were pushing the limits. Especially when I started hearing those voices in my head, "Go ahead. Go a little further. No one will ever know . . ."

Yeah, I knew we were going too far. I knew it. But I didn't stop! Neither of us did. We just kept going, giving more and more of our innocence to each other. Even though we both should have known better. Even though we both should have said "no."

Now, I feel guilty and dirty and emptied out and hollow. I feel used and afraid. I'm afraid to see 'em again because I'm afraid of what might happen. It'll be awkward for me because I feel so guilty and I won't know what to say. Are we supposed to pretend like it didn't happen? Are we gonna break up? What happens now?

If we keep going out I'm afraid we might pick up where we left off and end up doing the same thing all over again. Are we gonna struggle to connect at all from now on without getting physical?

Please help me, God. The inside of me is crying, begging for help. I wish I could go back in time and make a different choice, but I can't. Help my heart to start over again. Help my conscience find your forgiveness. Please. You're the God of second chances, and right now that's what I need. A second chance and wisdom to know what to do next.

Purify me, Jesus. Purify us both. Draw me closer to your heart. And let us give our relationship totally to you from now on . . .

"It's all about accepting God's forgiveness in your life, then forgiving yourself, believing that you really can change bad habits and receive God's healing for past wounds."

—rebecca st. james, christian singer and songwriter, from her book WAIT FOR ME

from the heart

here's what i want to tell my friend about how i'm feeling . . .

_____

_____

_____

here are the physical limits i need to set for my dating . . .

_____

_____

_____

in my own words, here's how i feel right now . . .

_____

_____

_____

deeper and further

Often the cycle of lust and going too far on a date starts with the eyes. Jesus points this out in Matthew 5:28. Read it for yourself. Jesus doesn't just ask us to pursue purity with our bodies, but also with our minds and imaginations. How does that make you feel? What does it do to the excuse, "Well, at least we didn't go all the way"? What choices do you have to make as a result of reading this verse?

"God wants you to be holy, so you should keep clear of all sexual sin. Then each of you will control your body and live in holiness and honor—not in lustful passion as the pagans do, in their ignorance of God and his ways."

1 Thessalonians 4:3-5

WHEN David was confronted with his sin with Bathsheba, he felt ashamed. When Peter realized he'd denied Jesus a third time just as Jesus had predicted, he felt ashamed. When we mess up today, we feel stinging, lingering regrets too—we feel ashamed just like they did.

Shame is natural when you know there are such things as right and wrong, good and bad. And the more clearly you know what's right, the more deeply you'll feel ashamed of your wrongs. Here's how one author put it:

Let there be tears for the wrong things you have done. Let there be sorrow and deep grief. Let there be sadness instead of laughter, and gloom instead of joy. (James 4:9)

Why would James suggest that we feel bad, sad, gloomy and sorrowful? Because that's how God feels about our wrongs. And Jesus wants us to view our sins more and more from God's perspective.

It's only when we look honestly at our lives and our sin that we'll go to God for healing and forgiveness. According to Ephesians 5:12, *"It is shameful even to talk about the things that ungodly people do in secret."*

And yet, for those who trust in the Lord, shame is erased by the grace of forgiveness.

> "If you are humble nothing will touch you, neither praise nor disgrace, because you know what you are."
>
> —mother teresa (1910-1997), winner of the 1979 nobel peace prize

from the gut

Oh, man. I've really done it this time. There's a lump in my throat and a lump in my heart and I'm nervous and scared and sorry and each of these feelings is like a huge beast that's ready to swallow me up.

Sometimes when I do something wrong I try to make up for it or I act good for awhile to try and make it all even out somehow. I know that's not how you look at it, I know I can't really balance out the scales, but it's just natural to try and make up for—to make amends for—our wrongs.

Anyway, this time I don't feel like there's enough good in the whole world to make up for it. I really blew it. Forgive me! I was wrong! I was so wrong. And I'm sorry! I don't have any excuses. I should have known better and now I just want to hide. I'm so ashamed I can hardly stand it.

That's all I can say. I don't have any good reasons why I did it. I don't have any defense. All I ask for is forgiveness, a fresh start and a clean slate.

You burn away and refine and cleanse and purify. You don't heat water and form it into awkward chunks of glistening ice. But you set it free from itself to fly and arise and taste the air and enter the heavens as mist and cloud.

I am the water, O Spirit; be to me the flame! And when I'm tempted, melt me and change me into a vapor that's caught up in your winds and blown toward the highest realms of your love where there is no more shame, only freedom and forgiveness and peace. And grace . . .

from the heart

God, this is why i'm feeling so ashamed . . .

_____

_____

_____

_____

_____

_____

Spirit, this is how i need you to cleanse my thoughts . . .

_____

_____

_____

_____

_____

_____

Jesus, this is what i need you to do for me right now . . .

_____

_____

_____

_____

_____

_____

deeper and further

Since Christ has taken our sins away, we can be confident that God isn't ashamed of us or embarrassed of us at all. And because of this new relationship with God, our entire situation has changed. Check out the good news in Hebrews 4:15, 16. How much confidence can we have when approaching God's throne? How does that affect your relationship with God? How does that make you feel?

"Those who look to him for help will be radiant with joy; no shadow of shame will darken their faces."

Psalm 34:5

prayers
for
girls

the popularity game

OKAY God, you want all of my life, all of my heart and soul and strength. And I tell others they should love you with their whole heart, too. But yet, how I wish they would love me, and think good things about me and admire me!

I want from them what you want from them—their thoughts and love and devotion. Yet when they give to you what you ask for (and leave no room for admiring me) then I feel hurt and slighted!

> "Alas, I have always wanted to impress others; I am eager for their approval. I long to be loved. I crave popularity. I make an idol of friendship and esteem by striving to occupy my neighbour's thoughts and to possess his heart."
> —francois de fenelon (1651-1715), priest, author and christian mystic

My pride is so overwhelming, God, that I want to hold the place of honor in their hearts when it's been reserved for you!

Notice me! It is the cry of my heart. Notice me! It is the call of my soul. Oh, how lost I am and how blind I am thinking only of myself; desiring only what's best for myself; focused only on my own future in a world so full of hurting, lonely souls!

Change me, O Spirit! Let me become oblivious to the opinions of others and seek only to honor and glorify you!

> "We all desire to live imaginary lives in the minds of other people."
> —blaise pascal (1623-1662), scientist, mathematician and philosopher

"in" but not "of" the world

*How am I supposed to live in this world but not of it? What does **that** look like? How can I rise above the things of this life? How can I pull apart from the ways of the world? The world is so enticing. I fall in love with its illusions so easily. Why do I wrap my heart around such fragile useless things?*

And how can I do that while still engaging my culture, embracing my friends and entering into relationships that matter without being drawn away from you?

How did you do it, Jesus? People loved hanging out with you. You totally accepted them without ever justifying their lifestyles or making light of their sins. You loved 'em out of this world and beyond themselves and into God's kingdom. How did you do that? And more importantly, how can I do it, too? Show me, O God. Take me along the path of "in" but not "of." Set me apart and raise me above the things that are meaningless to you . . .

"And now, Lord, with your help, I shall become myself."
—soren kierkegaard (1813-1855), theologian and philosopher

from the heart

God, i just really wish these people would like me . . .

_____
_____
_____
_____
_____
_____

God, more than being popular i'd like you to help me to become . . .

_____
_____
_____
_____
_____
_____

God, here's what i need to remember about popularity . . .

_____

_____

_____

_____

_____

_____

deeper and further

Jesus promised his followers that they wouldn't be popular with the world at all. In fact, read Matthew 10:22 and describe what kind of treatment they were supposed to expect. Why do you think that is? How does knowing that make you feel?

"Don't you realize that friendship with this world makes you an enemy of God? I say it again, that if your aim is to enjoy this world, you can't be a friend of God."

James 4:4

I'VE been stung.

I thought it was a butterfly walking on my arm. I could feel the gentle toes of friendship and trust so I didn't pull away. And before I realized what happened, I got stung. In the heart.

Because it wasn't a butterfly at all. It was a wasp in disguise.

And it hurts. It hurts mostly because I don't just feel wounded—wounds I can take. But wounds from someone this close to me are hard to handle. I feel violated and angry and sore and vengeful all at the same time. Here's what I wanna ask the person who hurt me: "How could you backstab me like that? How could you deceive me and lead me along and then totally betray me?!"

I'll be honest—I wanna get back at 'em.

Because I trusted that person! I trusted 'em with my feelings and the things that matter most in my life. And now I've been stung and I don't wanna trust again. Ever.

I need healing. Not just from the pain of being stabbed in the back, but from the feeling of being stabbed in the heart.

I know I'll be tempted not to trust again. I know I'll feel like hiding away and letting myself get all eaten up with bitterness and anger and resentment. I know I'll try to shield my feelings from being touched. But that's just another kind of prison.

Healing—of the heart and soul and spirit. That's what I need. Take the stinger out. And make the swelling go away so I can love that person again . . .

> "He that cannot forgive others breaks the bridge over which he must pass himself; for every man has need to be forgiven."
> —thomas fuller (1608-1661), english historian and clergyman

from the heart

God, here's the name of the person who hurt me:

_____

here's why i feel so betrayed . . .

_____
_____
_____
_____

here's how i'm gonna change my attitude so you can teach me to forgive . . .

_____
_____
_____
_____

deeper and further

Judas.

The name alone brings to mind images of deceit, betrayal and treachery. Take a look at Matthew 26:48-50. Even with such an intimate betrayal, what did Jesus call Judas? What does that tell you about Jesus' love? Jesus understands what you're going through. Talk to him about your situation in your own words, right now.

"Get rid of all bitterness, rage, anger, harsh words, and slander, as well as all types of malicious behavior. Instead, be kind to each other, tenderhearted, forgiving one another, just as God through Christ has forgiven you."

Ephesians 4:31, 32

GOD, I don't know why you made us so that we could care so much about someone and then end up getting hurt so deeply.

It's like my boyfriend spent all this time learning exactly what would hurt me the most. He led me on to think he really cared about me and then he just dumped all this pain into my heart like he didn't care at all.

I never knew I could ache this much for things to be back like they were. But I do.

Did you ever really think that dating and courtship and marriage could actually work? I mean, bringing two of us together you had to know there'd be struggles, right? And scars? And fights? And disappointments? And pain? So much pain!

Why couldn't you have designed it so that we weren't always hurting each other? Why couldn't you have made it so that we could be close and intimate without being so easily wounded and afraid and so deeply hurt?

I don't know if I should complain to you or burst into tears. Sometimes I feel like doing both. And I don't even think I want any answers. All I really want is someone who won't let me down. Someone like you, God. So just hear me, and don't walk away or shake your head or sigh or roll your eyes or cut me off in mid-sentence or swear at me under your breath.

I just need you right now to hold me and listen.

Hold me. It hurts so much. Just hold me . . .

> "Thank you for breaking my heart . . . you've only made me stronger."
>
> —anonymous

from the heart

this is the name of the guy who hurt me:

_____

these are the things that hurt the most . . .

_____

_____

_____

_____

_____

these are the ways i need you to help me . . .

_____

_____

_____

_____

_____

deeper and further

When you're hurting, check out Psalm 9:9, 10 and Psalm 22:1-5.
When you need help with emotional healing, check out Psalm
25:16-21 and Psalm 27:7-10.
When you need to learn to trust again, take a look at Psalm 22:9-
11 and Psalm 25:1-5.

*"The LORD is close to the brokenhearted; he rescues those who are
crushed in spirit."*

Psalm 34:18

GOD, I've been hurt. You know who it was and what they did. You know how deeply it ripped at my feelings. And God, I gotta tell you, part of me likes holding onto the hurt. Part of me likes nurturing the pain and letting my anger simmer. Part of me wants to say, "Okay. That's it. You blew it and I'm not gonna forgive you. Not now and not ever. Your second chances are over. Our friendship is over."

And, even though there's a sense of satisfaction in feeling that way, deep inside I know that part of me dies with every grudge I carry.

Some girls I know could hold onto a grudge forever. And I'm tempted to do that, too.

God, forgive me for my bitterness and help me to forgive like Jesus did—fully, completely, forever. From the heart . . .

Change me from an unforgiving, angry girl into a loving and forgiving person. It's not natural for me to forgive. Most of the time I'd rather not! But God, make the change deep inside me so that it becomes natural. Help me live in your direction, rather than always raging against what you have to say.

Thanks for listening . . .

"We must develop and maintain the capacity to forgive. He who is devoid of the power to forgive is devoid of the power to love. There is some good in the worst of us and some evil in the best of us. When we discover this, we are less prone to hate our enemies."
—martin luther king, jr. (1929-1968), pastor, civil rights leader and nobel peace prize recipient

from the heart

here's the wrong that i don't want to forgive . . .

_____

_____

_____

here's why i'm tempted to carry this grudge . . .

_____

_____

_____

here's what i need you to do to help me to forgive . . .

_____

_____

_____

deeper and further

Read what Jesus had to say about forgiving others in Matthew 6:14, 15. Why do you think it's so important to God that we forgive others? What happens if we refuse to forgive them? Do you need to ask for God's help to forgive someone right now?

"I am warning you! If another believer sins, rebuke him; then if he repents, forgive him. Even if he wrongs you seven times a day and each time turns again and asks forgiveness, forgive him."

Luke 17:3, 4

O GOD, I wish there were some way to know for sure. To know if I've finally found out what it means to love someone. I don't mean "love" like I love you or my mom or a slice of pizza or a roller coaster ride. I mean the real thing . . . you know.

Whenever I'm with this guy I just want the day to last forever or the night to go on and on. We get lost in each other's eyes! And whenever we touch, it's electric. It seems like time stands still and I get dizzy just thinking about being with him! I can hardly control myself. Everything is so alive!

I wonder if you can ever know for sure if you're in love. Adults are always talking like you can. I'm just glad you gave us this. Whatever it is!

Maybe it's kinda like you. I mean, I know you're there and I know I love you, but there's something mysterious about it, too. It's not something I can prove. It's just something I know is true. Like you're always just out of reach, but always within my grasp.

Love.

Could I really be in love? It's weird to talk to you about this, but I know you don't think I'm stupid for not knowing. Thanks for sharing my excitement, whatever this is I'm feeling. God, be our guide, wherever this leads. Thanks for listening. Thanks for caring . . .

> "Life has taught us that love does not consist in gazing at each other but in looking outward together in the same direction."
> —antoine de saint-exupery (1900-1944), pilot, poet and author

from the heart

here's the name of the guy who has stolen my heart:

_____

here's why i think i might be falling in love . . .

_____

_____

_____

in my own words, here's how i'm feeling right now . . .

_____

_____

_____

deeper and further

Real love involves feelings as well as commitment. When Joseph found out that his fiancée Mary was pregnant, he knew it wasn't his baby. He struggled with how to respond. Read Matthew 1:18-25 to see how that all played out. What was he potentially giving up by staying in that relationship? What does that tell you about his love for Mary? (For a clue see 1 John 3:18).

One of the keys to real love is a willingness to sacrifice on behalf of your beloved. Are you willing to do that for the guy you like? Is he willing to do that for you? When you stop thinking about what you can get out of a relationship, and can't wait to put more into it, you're on the pathway toward true love.

"We know what real love is because Christ gave up his life for us."
1 John 3:16

when i'm tempted to gossip

GOD, gossiping doesn't seem like a big deal compared to a lot of other stuff. It's just so natural and easy and I end up doing it so much without even realizing it. God, forgive me! Make me sensitive to the feelings and reputations of others. Help me to not only refuse to gossip about others, but refuse to listen to gossip, too.

I don't want anything to do with the stuff you despise . . .

when growing up is freaking me out

God, things are changing so fast! I'm trying to figure out who I am and what I stand for and what role I'm supposed to have in this world.

And then there's driving and dating and college to think about and so many changes happening in my body. God, I'm becoming a woman and it's scary, but so exciting, too! I'm kinda freaked out by all that growing up involves.

Help me to hold onto a childlike faith as I become a woman of God. And be with me through the journey . . .

when i find out i'm pregnant

O God, I can't believe it! What do I do now? Where can I turn? I don't know what to do! I can't believe I'm really pregnant!

Now I guess I gotta decide what to do. I know people say it's not a baby yet, but God, that can't be true, can it? I mean, everyone knows it's a baby. Calling it a fetus and pretending it's not human is just a way of trying to escape the responsibility of actually carrying it to term. Because when you admit you're carrying a baby, abortion would be unthinkable. It would be the same as murder . . .

God, I don't want to have an abortion, but I don't know if I'm brave enough to do the right thing! Help me! Show me where to turn and who to talk to. Help me make sense of this and somehow choose the right direction to walk.

Wipe away my tears, God. I need you more than I ever have before!

from the heart

God, here's a tough decision i'm facing right now . . .

_____
_____
_____
_____
_____
_____

God, here's what i need from you in my life . . .

_____
_____
_____
_____
_____
_____

Lord, here's the stuff i struggle with the most . . .

_____
_____
_____
_____
_____
_____

Read James 3:1-12. What do these verses have to say about gossiping? Find three warnings in these verses about the use of your tongue. What does James compare a tongue to? Now read Luke 6:45. What's the secret to having a mouth that honors God? Where does Jesus say our words bubble out of? What do you need to do about that in your life?

> "The LORD your God is with you, he is mighty to save. He will take great delight in you, he will quiet you with his love, he will rejoice over you with singing."
>
> *Zephaniah 3:17 NIV*

JESUS never taught people to be ashamed of their bodies, only the shameful things they did with their bodies. Each of us is uniquely and incredibly valued by God. Here's what King David said about the subject:

You made all the delicate, inner parts of my body and knit me together in my mother's womb. Thank you for making me so wonderfully complex! Your workmanship is marvelous—and how well I know it. (Psalm 139:13, 14)

We don't often think of our bodies as wonderfully complex or marvelously made. We tend to feel like maybe God made a mistake somewhere along the line when he made us because we compare ourselves to others. You'll never win when you play the comparison game because ultimately, you'll always find someone more slim, gorgeous, attractive, smart or athletic than you.

Maybe that's why God doesn't want us to compare ourselves with others, or to find our self-worth in how we look. As believers our entire identity should be caught up in our relationship with Christ—we're so precious to him that he even chooses to live within us (see 1 Corinthians 6:19).

"I think women see me on the cover of magazines and think I never have a pimple or bags under my eyes. You have to realize that's after two hours of hair and makeup, plus retouching. Even I don't wake up looking like Cindy Crawford."

—cindy crawford, supermodel

from the gut

God, I just don't get why you made me the way you did. I'm so ashamed of how I look.

I see other girls and they're totally gorgeous and their bodies are perfect and then I look at myself. I glance into the mirror and all I see are a nose that looks too big and a body that's way too fat. I feel ugly!

Oh, how I want to feel like a princess! Graceful and gorgeous and confident. And lovely. I want to feel lovely! That's the deep desire of my heart. Yet, I don't feel like there's anything special about me at all.

The most amazing truth I think I've ever heard in all the Bible is that you care for me as is. You love me the way I am, not as I might someday be. Could that really be true?

*Do you really love me? Did you really design me like this? Is it true you planned for me to be this way and look like this . . . because of your great **love** for me? Did you really shape me in the center of your heart? If so, then why is it so hard for me to feel pretty? Why is it so easy for me to compare myself to everyone else?*

Keep me from the trap of trying to be someone I'm not or of always looking down on myself. Help me to value, respect and appreciate my body as much as you do . . .

from the heart

these are the parts of myself that are the hardest to accept . . .

_____

_____

_____

_____

here are some ways you have made me beautiful . . .

_____

_____

_____

_____

here's why i think you made me the way you did . . .

_____

_____

_____

_____

deeper and further

The church is called the bride of Christ. Paul says that Jesus died for the church (i.e. believers) to make her beautiful and holy. Read it for yourself in Ephesians 5:25-27. All those who believe in Christ are part of the bride of Christ. In these verses, how does Paul describe your true spiritual beauty in the sight of God? How does that make you feel? How does it change your attitude about your own loveliness?

"Don't be concerned about the outward beauty that depends on fancy hairstyles, expensive jewelry, or beautiful clothes. You should be known for the beauty that comes from within, the unfading beauty of a gentle and quiet spirit, which is so precious to God."
1 Peter 3:3, 4

prayers
for
guys

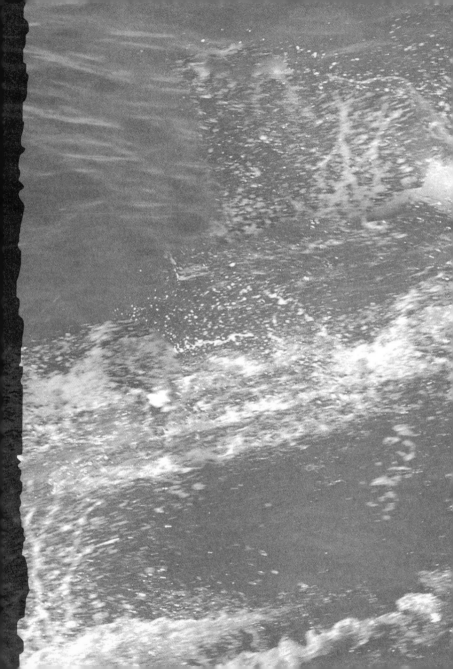

A JELLYFISH has no backbone. It floats around in the water, drifting wherever the tide takes it—even if that means being deposited on shore. And once on land, a jellyfish loses its shape and lays in the sand in a helpless blob. A jellyfish is totally at the mercy of its environment.

Jesus was no jellyfish.

He not only went against the flow, but he did it in shark-infested waters. Nothing could stop him or deter him from pursuing his mission of bringing honor to his Father. Not criticism. Not threats. Not intimidation. Not even torture. He stood up for his beliefs and he never backed down, even though it eventually cost him his life.

Two other men, both criminals, were also led out with him to be executed. When they came to the place called the Skull, there they crucified him, along with the criminals—one on his right, the other on his left. Jesus said, "Father, forgive them, for they do not know what they are doing." (Luke 23:32-34 NIV)

Jesus confronted adversity with backbone and answered persecution with love. When things didn't go his way, when everyone turned against him and even his friends deserted him, he responded with courage, faith and patient endurance. Jesus was more like a boulder in the surf than a jellyfish in the sand. He never gave up and he never gave in.

Through his power today, we can stand up to the currents of culture, too. God isn't interested in jellyfish. His followers need to make the choice once and for all to do things God's way and follow him. Wherever that leads. Just like Jesus did.

"Real integrity is doing the right thing, knowing that nobody's going to know whether you did it or not."
—oprah winfrey, actress, producer and television and radio host

God, give me the guts to do the right thing and make the right choices, even when it's not easy, even when part of me doesn't want to! Help me to stand up for you, even when it's not popular, even when it means standing alone.

If God is on my side, who can be against me? If God is fighting for me, how could I ever lose? If God is with me, how could I ever be alone? If God is within me, how could I lack any good thing? If God is my guide and my pathway, how could I ever be led astray? If God has reserved a place for me in Heaven, how could I ever lose my inheritance?

I live as if I'm in control of my future. I act as if the choices I make in this life are really all that there is. How stupid! How foolish to be in love with the mist rather than the mountain! To try to cling to the vapor as it slips through my hand when Heaven and all of its promises call to me. Remind me, God, how brief my life is! Show me clearly how closely death snaps at my heels and how each choice I make really matters! Who am I gonna live for, myself or you?

I've made my choice. Now help me live it out . . .

from the heart

God, these are the reasons why it's so tough to follow you . . .

_____

_____

_____

_____

_____

_____

God, i know i shouldn't be afraid of this stuff, but i am anyway . . .

_____

_____

_____

_____

_____

_____

God, here's what i need you to give me the guts to do . . .

_____

_____

_____

_____

_____

_____

deeper and further

Read Revelation 21:8. Why do you think God leads off his "directory of the damned" with cowards? What does that tell you about the kind of conviction God requires of his followers? Where is the only source of that kind of courage and resolve? Have you tapped into God's strength yet today? If not, do so right now by asking him to empower and equip you to do what you need to do.

"So you must never be ashamed to tell others about our Lord."
2 Timothy 1:8

MAN, the way I lose my temper scares me. It's not just that I'm a little impatient with people, it's way beyond that. I mean, my anger rises up in me like a storm. I end up blasting anyone who gets in my path, and it's usually the people who are closest to me that get hurt the worst. My words turn into clubs that bruise their hearts!

And the scary thing is, I can't seem to control it on my own. Someday I'm gonna do something that I'm really gonna regret. I'm gonna hurt someone in a way that can't be fixed. God, help me to not only control my anger, but to find healthy ways to let loose steam. Maybe in sports, or lifting weights, or going for a walk or whatever. Open up the doors I need opened and show me the way.

Help me to stay angry at the things you get angry at—hypocrisy, hatred, cheating, mocking. Stuff like that. But help me to be patient with other people. It's not right to get mad at stuff just because it's not convenient for me. Show me the difference. And then, be the Lord of my anger. Be the Lord of my whole life.

Help me to keep my anger from boiling over. And when I feel like screaming, when life hurts and no one seems to notice me, then listen to me, let me vent and lead me in the right direction again. Lord, help me to control my anger instead of letting it control me . . .

"You wouldn't like me when I'm angry."

—dr. bruce banner, the incredible hulk

from the heart

these are the things that make me the most angry . . .

_____

_____

_____

_____

here are the ways i've tried to deal with my anger that haven't worked . . .

_____

_____

_____

_____

here is the person (or group of people) i really need to work on being patient with:

_____

deeper and further

There were times when Jesus lost his patience. There were times when he got really angry with people. But whenever he got angry, he did it for good reasons. Read Romans 1:18, 19 and John 2:13-16. What are the things that anger God?

The Bible doesn't even tell us not to get angry. It just says that we should be sure that the things we're angry at are the same things God would get angry at. And it says we shouldn't let anger lead us into sin. It's a fine line, but with God's help you can walk it.

"'In your anger do not sin': Do not let the sun go down while you are still angry."

Ephesians 4:26 NIV

GOD, for a long time now you've known about my struggle. You've watched me get buried in a set of circumstances that always lead me to the same place. One step at a time, one choice at a time, I just keep going past the point of no return.

And it's been a long time since I've cried about it or felt as bad as I probably should about doing it. Oh, I used to. At first it really bothered me. But slowly I sank deeper and deeper under the control of this thing until I couldn't say "no" anymore.

It's a trap that's always there. And I'm always on the edge, ready to slip over.

It hasn't gotten easier to deal with in time, but harder. I know other people deal with addictions, too. Drinking. Drugs. Sports. Each of us gets slowly sucked into different things. Working. Gambling. Internet porn. Soft and hard-core porn. Whatever. And you've helped them to say "no."

You've helped others break free. Now, help me. I don't wanna play games with you. And I don't wanna mess around with this thing. I need serious help here. And I need it now.

Change the direction of my life in big ways and small. I hand this addiction to you. Crush it and set me free. It's up to you now God. Keep your promise. Do your work in my life and help me . . .

"The first step to humility is to realize you are proud."
—c. s. lewis (1898-1963), author of the CHRONICLES OF NARNIA

from the heart

God, my biggest addiction is . . .

_____

_____

_____

God, i'm gonna take these steps to beat my addiction . . .

_____

_____

_____

_____

_____

Lord, help me to replace my addiction with things like . . .

_____

_____

_____

_____

_____

deeper and further

Paul was addicted to sin. He struggled with doing things he didn't even want to do, as if he were under their control. He asked, "Who will set me free from this body of death?" (Romans 7:24 NIV). To find out his answer, read the following verse. Then, turn to the same place Paul did for help.

"So, dear brothers and sisters, you have no obligation whatsoever to do what your sinful nature urges you to do. For if you keep on following it, you will perish. But if through the power of the Holy Spirit you turn from it and its evil deeds, you will live."

Romans 8:12, 13

KING David had a lot of enemies. His predecessor, Saul, tried for years to have him killed. The neighboring Philistines were always out to get him. Even his own son Absalom rose up against David and tried to take over his kingdom.

One time, when the Philistines captured David in Gath, he prayed these words:

They are always twisting what I say; they spend their days plotting ways to harm me. They come together to spy on me—watching my every step, eager to kill me. . . . For you have rescued me from death; you have kept my feet from slipping. So now I can walk in your presence, O God, in your life-giving light. (Psalm 56:5, 6, 13)

Jesus never guaranteed that the life of a believer would be carefree or easy. Life swells up around every one of us and sometimes it can be tough to keep our bearings. When David was surrounded, attacked and overwhelmed, he turned to God. And God rescued him. David felt like slipping, but his faith gave him a firm place to stand and his God gave him his presence and guidance.

Does it sometimes seem to you like people twist around what you say? Do they plot ways to hurt you? Do they spy on you, watching and waiting for you to mess up? Does life overwhelm you, too?

Reread the last half of the Scripture above. Who rescued David? How did David respond to God when God delivered him?

No matter who you are, there are gonna be times when life seems to overwhelm you. The problems seem too big, the questions seem too tough, the troubles seem too devastating. But God is bigger than your problems, questions and troubles. Turn to him like David did. And God will either guide you through the problems or remove them altogether. Either way, he'll rescue you and you can walk in God's presence just like David did.

from the gut

Man!

Why are they doing this to me? Why? Why is everything and everybody all lined up against me like this? What did I ever do to them? It's not fair that they treat me like this! It's not!

I'm sick of people accusing me of things and getting me in trouble and judging me. I feel like everyone is against me—that they're all ganging up on me and even people I trusted are out to get me.

It's a pretty hard place to be. It hurts to feel this way. Because there really isn't anywhere to turn. Sometimes I can connect with how David felt. Attacked. Spied on. Schemed against. You rescued him from life's problems. Now rescue me!

God, I really like being liked. But remind me that even if others reject me, you never will.

I guess Jesus turned to you, too, God, when he felt this way. And he had more reasons to feel ganged up on than I will ever have.

God, if you can make it right, that would be cool. But if you decide not to, then help me to know that you're bigger than my problems. Help me to remember that you're on my side, even if no one else is. Even if I have no one else to turn to, I can turn to you.

Thanks . . .

from the heart

here are the names of the people who are out to get me . . .

_____

_____

_____

_____

_____

_____

here's how i feel when i get ganged up on . . .

_____

_____

_____

_____

_____

_____

with your help, here's what i'm gonna do the next time i start
feeling this way . . .

_____

_____

_____

_____

_____

_____

deeper and further

King David often wrote about being alone or attacked or
surrounded. Read all the way through Psalm 56. Where did he find
the strength to keep going? What truths helped him get through the
tough times? How will these truths help you, too?

*"Turn to me and have mercy on me, for I am alone and in deep
distress."*

Psalm 25:16

JESUS uttered some pretty tough words. Often he drew a line in the sand, like he did when he said these words:

Anyone who isn't helping me opposes me, and anyone who isn't working with me is actually working against me. (Luke 11:23)

There it is. Jesus is the line in the sand and all the world stands on one side of him or the other. There's no in-between. No way to abstain. No way to sit out. You vote by your life. Either you're for him or against him. That's the way it is. So here's the question: Where do you stand?

from the gut

wake me up

God, I gotta admit some stuff here.

I like being comfortable. I like trendy clothes and a cool car and living in a nice house and all that stuff. And I like it when other people notice that I have these things. I like doing what I want when I want, buying and eating and wearing the things I like. I like all that stuff.

Being comfortable has become so much a part of my life that I rarely even question it or consider that it might not please you. Sometimes I look down on other people and on their shameful desires and shallow pursuits and their selfish goals. But meanwhile, they're looking down on me for the same things because we're all lured by similar voices and ensnared by the same kinds of enticing promises.

Jesus, you warned us about becoming too comfortable in this world! You warned us about being lulled to sleep and lured away by the bright lights and flashy promises and nice things of this world. Wake me up! Shake me loose and help me to give my all to you!

God, most of the time I don't bring you my best at all. I just hand you my leftovers. Leftover time. Leftover energy. Leftover dreams. Leftover money. Leftover devotion. But that's not how I want it to be anymore. I wanna bring you my best. I wanna bring you all of myself. To do with as you please.

Here I am, God. Do your work in me and work your will in my life . . .

help me serve you

You've set me free. I can disobey you if I want to, but my desire is to serve you instead. You've set me free, now let me live in the freedom of the moment without regrets or fear or holding back any of myself. Here is what really makes me happy—to be close to you. Now that you've set me free, I no longer desire freedom. All I desire is oneness with you, closeness to you . . . not doing what I want, but doing what you want . . . not going my own way, but going yours.

That's the true path of freedom.

Now, show me the difference between being a genuine follower of you, and a deceived lover of this world. Do what you must in my soul . . .

sweep through me

God, I don't understand! I know that I long for you, yet the closer you come to me the more I retreat!

Is it because you shed so much light on my soul that I can't stand to look upon it? Is it because the closer you come to me, the clearer I hear you calling and the more I realize all the suffering I inflict? The more I realize how much you ask of me, the more I realize how little I've given to you in the past!

Sweep through me, Holy Spirit! Where I hold back part of myself, show me that blessing comes from giving you my all. Help me to let go of all the shallow and selfish goals that I cling to so tightly. Open my hands to receive whatever you choose to give. No more holding back. No more putting it off. Here I am. Right now, Lord.

Sweep through me . . .

> "So no one can become my disciple without giving up everything for me."
> —Jesus of nazareth (luke 14:33)

from the heart

here are three things that have been holding me back from a total commitment . . .

1. _____
   _____

2. _____
   _____

3. _____
   _____

here are the changes i'm gonna make in my life to bring you more glory . . .

_____

_____

_____

_____

_____

_____

here's one specific thing i'm gonna do to put you first in my life . . .

_____

_____

_____

_____

_____

_____

Thomas often gets a bad rap for doubting that Jesus was really alive after he arose. People have referred to him as "doubting Thomas" ever since. But check out his conviction in John 11:13-16. What was he ready to do for Jesus? Does that sound like a guy full of doubt to you? How does that make you feel about your doubts? Can God still use you?

"And so, dear brothers and sisters, I plead with you to give your bodies to God. Let them be a living and holy sacrifice—the kind he will accept. When you think of what he has done for you, is this too much to ask?"

Romans 12:1

Job, one of the richest and most influential men of the ancient world, wanted to stay sexually pure. Read Job 31:1. What did Job do to avoid drifting into sexual sin? Did his choice affect just his behavior, or his imagination as well? How can you tell? What kind of covenant do you need to make with your eyes?

"But remember that the temptations that come into your life are no different from what others experience. And God is faithful. He will keep the temptation from becoming so strong that you can't stand up against it. When you are tempted, he will show you a way out so that you will not give in to it."

1 Corinthians 10:13

when i break up with my girlfriend

GOD, relationships can get messy. People get hurt, feelings get trashed. Emotions get trampled. That's what happened to us. Sometimes it was my fault, and sometimes it was hers. Things just didn't work out, I guess.

Either way, whosever fault it was, I'm carrying around a lot of questions right now. There was a lot of fallout. And now I'm second guessing some of the things that were said and done and wondering if things would have played out differently if maybe I'd acted a little differently at times.

I guess sometimes things just aren't meant to be. I mean, interests change and you move on. I guess what I'm trying to ask is, heal the wounds that are left over, erase the bitterness, calm the anger. Help us both move on in a healthy way. It's not that I want to forget her, or get back at her or whatever. I just need help figuring this all out.

God, please heal us both so we don't carry any permanent scars from this mess . . .

> "Nothing takes the taste out of peanut butter quite like unrequited love."
> —charlie brown, comic strip character

when a girl rejects me

Oh man. I feel like such a loser.

God, you already know how it all went down so I don't really have to tell you. But I feel so rejected and like such an idiot for feeling the way I feel about her, for even thinking she'd wanna be with me.

What are you supposed to do when you feel like this? When you get totally rejected? Just pick up and move on? Pretend like nothing happened? I can't do that! It hurts too much!

It's like all my confidence and self-image were wrapped up in her saying "yes" to me, but she said the other word instead. The word that ripped me apart.

"No."

Help me out here, God. Do what you need to do in my heart and give me the guts to keep going and to find my acceptance and identity in you rather than in some girl. Thanks . . .

from the heart

Jesus, here are my questions about relationships . . .

_____
_____
_____
_____
_____
_____

here's how i'm feeling right now . . .

_____
_____
_____
_____
_____
_____

here's the name of the girl i'm having problems with:

_____

According to Proverbs 31:30, what kind of a girl should you be looking for? Where can you find a girl like that to connect with? Why are girls like that so rare? Why are they totally worth the wait?

"The LORD says, 'I will guide you along the best pathway for your life. I will advise you and watch over you.'"

Psalm 32:8